SHOOT, HOST, POST

Virtual/Video Tours, Live Virtual Open Houses, & Social Media Strategy for Real Estate Agents

Tracy Ramsay, M.A., Realtor® & Brie E. Anderson
Video Estate Agent, LLC Wichita, KS

Printed in the United States of America
First Printing 2020
First Edition 2020

978-17352888-4-0

SHOOT, HOST, POST

Acknowledgements

We would like to thank Cindy Carnahan and The Carnahan Group, ReeceNichols South Central Kansas. We would also like to thank Kathy Rosell and Katie Brown from The Carnahan Group for their participation and willingness to ask questions, learn, and serve as our sounding boards during this process. Their contributions formed the foundation for our course as well as this book.

Tracy would like to give a special thank you to Frank Messina from Real Living, Messina & Associates for generously and lovingly sharing your almost 50 years of real estate experience in your New York-Italian manner. Your leadership and commitment to excellence have made a lasting impact on the real estate industry in Duluth, MN and beyond. Not every turtle makes it to the top of the real estate fencepost, but it helps when you've been climbing since Moby Dick was a guppy.

We'd also like to thank friends and family who cheered us on even when we were ignoring them, chatting their ears off, or making them listen to us practice (especially in quarantine) - WE LOVE YOU!

Table of Contents

Preface

I'll never forget my first assignment as a newly licensed real estate agent, way back in the fall of 1998. My broker, Frank Messina, had just signed the paperwork to list a vacant house, and he wanted me to work as his assistant. Not only would he be teaching me the "right" way to work a listing, but I'd be taking and editing photos, developing film (1998, remember?), filling out paperwork, and - if I was lucky – meeting a buyer at the open house that was planned for Sunday.

I remember I was so excited at the thought of finally making some real money. I checked out the company camera, jumped in my car, drove up to the listing, and stood across the street taking photos of the exterior. I then went to a nearby Walgreens to get the photos developed, even paying extra to get them ASAP. I was so proud of how efficient I was, and I couldn't wait to show Frank the fruits of my labor.

Photos in hand, I knocked on Frank's door and proudly handed him the envelope, announcing at the same time that I was going to go ahead and get started on the paperwork. As I exited his office, I looked behind me to sneak a peek of him going through the photos. As he did, his pleasant demeanor changed, and his face turned red.

"What is this?" he asked in a high-pitched screech?

My head sunk. My ego deflated. Sheepishly, I walked over to glance at the photo he was holding.

"What is this?" he said, louder this time.
"It's a picture of the house you just listed," I said, unsure of what sort of answer he was looking for. "Isn't it?"

Doubt crept in. Did I get the address wrong and photograph the wrong house? Frank was beet red and looked as if his head might pop off if he didn't get the answer he wanted. Finally, he turned the photo towards me and shoved it in my face.

"THIS!" he barked, pointing to a car parked in front of the house. "What is this?"

I looked again, and answered hesitantly, "Um, it's a car?"

"YES! You got it. It's a car!" he exclaimed. "Are we in the business of selling cars? No, we sell houses! If you want to sell cars, go work at a car dealership!"

At this point, I thought Frank was a little crazy. I mean, I couldn't believe he was making such a big deal out of a car parked in the street. What was I supposed to do? Tow it? As he stared at me, huffing and puffing, I began to consider whether or not I'd made the wrong decision by choosing this real estate brokerage. After all, I wasn't getting paid for any of this grunt work! On top of all that, I felt more than a little attacked and was eager to come to my own defense.

I told Frank that I was sorry, but that I didn't think the picture I took was *that* bad. I also told him that I felt he was overreacting, and that a car being parked in the shot just wasn't that big of a deal.

As I quickly learned, that was the wrong thing to say.

Frank immediately replied that not only was I wrong but that it was indeed a big deal. After all, he wasn't in the business of training either car salespeople or overconfident agents who didn't want to learn. Agents that cut corners were a dime a dozen, and he simply didn't need them at his company. Not only did he have standards he wanted maintained (ouch!), but our clients were trusting us to present their homes in the best possible light.

As Frank continued explaining, I watched the natural color start to return to his face. Clearly, this was a teaching moment, and I just hadn't realized it yet. He explained that the biggest difference between being a mediocre agent and being a wildly successful agent was the small amount of time spent **thinking about** and **planning** simple tasks. Had I only taken a couple of extra minutes to do both, I could have saved time, money, and effort. As soon as I learned that one lesson, Frank said, my real estate career would take off.

So, I ate my humble pie and drove back to the listing to take photos...again. However, this time, I took five extra minutes to plan my shots carefully, thinking about how I would want the house to look if I were the one selling it. When I was finished, I drove back to Walgreens and used my own money to get the photos developed. I then went back to the office, where I got Frank's approval on the new batch of photos. To my delight, he invited me to work the open house that Sunday, where I officially met my first buyer.

Now, I would love to tell you that I spend the rest of my real estate career thinking ahead and planning every second of my day. Of course, that's not entirely true. There were many times I was too busy to put the extra care into a project. What I can say is that every time I DID take the extra time to prepare, I never regretted doing so - even when there was a learning curve involved.

It is that positive energy that led me to write this book. After all, I understand that video is new for most of you and that there will be a learning curve to overcome. However, I can promise you that we did our best to consider every question, tip, and detail to make this project a success. Hopefully, it will help you become wildly successful on your own real estate journey.

Good luck!

Introduction

Nobody expects a pandemic, at least nobody except the scientists everyone ignores in those "killer virus" movies. Moreover, no real estate agent ever expected to say, "2020 will be the year I do business by virtual reality." But thanks to our new normal, we've all had to shift our thinking of what is real, what is temporary, and what is possible in the real estate business.

Now, I get that not everyone can quickly shift into seeing virtual sales as an opportunity. With the health concerns, stay-at-home orders, and social distancing, our comfortable, face-to-face industry turned virtual overnight, catching all of us (save the writers of *Outbreak)* off guard.

Suddenly, agents were meeting more clients on FaceTime than in person. Their Sunday open houses were replaced by virtual open houses, and they were expected to actively participate in videos over social media platforms that they never wanted to be on in the first place!

Understandably, many agents—especially the open house pros that invest hundreds or even thousands of dollars into professional photography —are annoyed at having to participate in this new virtual undertaking. I hear them asking, with resistance, "I already have professional virtual photography and use Matterport, so I don't understand why I need to get in front of the camera, take a video of myself showing the house, and post it online...only to risk making me look like an idiot."

This begs the question: do you really need to film your own virtual tours? Well, that depends. Do you want to attract more clients? Do you want to sell more houses? Do you want to make more money? Creating your own virtual tours can help you achieve all of those goals.

In fact, according to the National Association of Realtors®, over 90% of all buyers use the internet when shopping for a home. [1] This means the vast majority of people are sitting on their phone or at their computer, scrutinizing photos to see if the house is worth their time to go view in person. Normally, if a house looks interesting, they will also look at Google Earth and "drive" down the block, scoping out the neighbors. They'll then check out the Zillow "Zestimator" to see if the property is really worth the asking price. And, since the pandemic began, more and more people are flocking to the internet shopping for homes instead of going out.

Facetime and zoom calls have started replacing showings, and most Multiple Listing Services now include a "virtual tour" feature. These innovative tools allow agents to post their own virtual tours (as opposed to previously only professional tours) to help cut down on in-person showings. Buying homes without ever stepping foot in them has become commonplace, buyers are now being forced to trust photos, videos, and Realtors® for accurate information.[2]

What does all of this mean for real estate agents? It means clients may not get many chances, if any at all, to meet you in person. It means clients will want to see you in some way, so that they can get a feel for your personality and vibe. Can they trust you? Are you knowledgeable? Videos let them see and decide for themselves. In fact, clients are more likely to trust a video of you introducing yourself or footage of a happy client than a few sales-oriented paragraphs. Videos put a face to your business. They allow customers to feel they know you before deciding to work with you. And while we don't know whether this is a change for

---

[1] National Association of Realtors®. (2020). https://www.nar.realtor/.
[2] Taylor, Candace. "Coronavirus Has Some Buyers Purchasing Homes Without Setting Foot Inside Them," The Wall Street Journal, May 14, 2020, https://www.wsj.com/articles/coronavirus-has-some-buyers-purchasing-homes-without-setting-foot-inside-them

the better or not, we do know that - pandemic or not - video is here and here to stay.

To that point, statistics show that homes listed alongside video content get a much higher number of inquiries than those listed without photos or text alone. Why? Because people want to get a feel for the homes, the layout, the spaces and rooms - even the neighborhood. After all, it's much easier to watch a video than to look at photographs or read descriptions. Another benefit of using video content is that it saves you loads of time. Once you make a video, it's made, and you don't need to do it again. You can simply post or add a link to the relevant videos without repeating something you've already explained IN that video. Each video can be placed, viewed, and shared in multiple places 24/7. Your videos are working for you all the time!

Here are some compelling facts about the benefits of posting even a single video per week:

- Homes listed with video get four times more inquiries compared to homes that were listed without video.[3]
- 85% of buyers and sellers prefer to work with an agent who uses video marketing techniques.[4]
- 75% of homeowners are more likely to list with an agent who uses video marketing to list their home.[5]

- 40% of Realtors® have seen an increase of over 40% in profits from the use of video marketing.[6]

We see the statistics related to video as indicating an exciting opportunity for you to shine and grow your business. Even with the

---

[3] Royster, Kathryn. "Real Estate Video Marketing's Biggest Return on Investment: High-Quality Community and Listing Videos Syndicated to YouTube, Shared on Social," Inman, July 7, 2014, https://www.inman.com/next/by-the-numbers-how-to-focus-your-video-marketing-for-the-biggest-return-on-investment/.

[4] Royster, "Real Estate Video Marketing," Inman

[5] Wong, Rachel. "A Realtors®® Guide to Video Marketing," RESAAS Blog (RESAAS, June 22, 2017), https://blog.resaas.com/articles/video-marketing-guide-for-Realtors®-infographic.

[6] Wong, "Realtors® Guide," RESAAS Blog.of their busy schedules to see them in person. Virtual tours are versatile, innovative, and creative. Plus, they allow clients to do viewings on their own time, in their own space.

pandemic, there are relatively few agents doing their own virtual tours, and if they are, they are not being done very well. Instead, agents are racing through homes at a dizzying speed, forgetting key features, and ignoring factors like good sound or lighting. In many cases, you are left wondering why the agent even bothered at all. It's kind of like the pictures you see of an agent attempting to photograph a bathroom, but all you can see is the agent standing in front of the mirror with their camera.

Still, even after this pandemic has passed, there's simply no going back. Everything is going mobile. People want to view a dozen homes without scheduling, arranging, and taking time out

In this book, we are going to go over the different types of virtual tours, the benefits and drawbacks of each, and then actually teach you how to shoot, edit, and maximize those videos on social media. Since there is such a wide gap between what consumers want (demand) and what is being produced by most agents (supply), we feel now is the time for agents like YOU to fill the gap, give the customers what they want, and make more money!

By the end of this book, you should have all the equipment you need as well as valuable hands-on experience shooting and editing your own videos. You will also know the ins and outs of where and when to post your videos to maximize their potential and how to use social media to build your business. Get ready! You're about to embark on a business-booming adventure!

Section 1

INTRODUCTION TO VIDEO BASICS

Chapter 1

Types of Virtual Tours

There are three types of virtual tours: professional virtual tours, agent virtual tours/video tours, and live virtual open houses. Let's briefly look at what defines each type and discuss what they all do best.

Virtual tours are all the rage in real estate right now! Since the pandemic and the subsequent rise in virtual showings, more agents than ever are taking to their cell phones or relying on photographers to show their listings. That said, we all too often see the terms "virtual tour" and "video tour" being used synonymously.

Historically, the term "virtual tour" included a series of professional photographs set to music. As technology has evolved, however, video tours have also fallen under the category of virtual tours in many MLS systems. So, for the sake of this book and in an attempt to stay on trend, we are defining "virtual tours" as any type of photography or videography that shows a sequence of images of a house to create a virtual experience for the consumer. Moreover, we have broken them down into three categories.

Professional Virtual Tours

The professional virtual tour is the kind most often seen on Zillow or Realtor.com, and are always are taken and edited by hired photographers and videographers. Many virtual tours are just professional pictures put together in a slide show, while others are more elaborate 3D platforms that require special equipment or are subscription-based. Typically, the more elaborate the tour, the higher the price, as you'll pay for both professional photography / videography and editing. Professional virtual tours are the most expensive type of virtual tour, but when they are done well, they are usually polished enough to really attract people to a house.

PROS	CONS
• **Shiny look and feel loved by sellers and buyers**	• Expensive
• **Professionally-edited**	• Limited information shared with audience (generally)
• **Professionally-shot**	• Lacks personal touch
• **Less work required from the you**	• Can have a longer turnaround time

Agent Virtual/Video Tours

These are personalized, pre-recorded virtual tours of you, the agent, going through the house. Usually, they consist of you showing off the features you like and highlighting the most valuable selling points. These can be quick tours, similar to the professionally-shot tours, or they can be longer (providing you more time to elaborate on what you and the seller want featured).

Agent tours are especially helpful when highlighting a home's location or property, which often gets overlooked in professional virtual tours. They also provide an opportunity for you to introduce yourself to potential buyers. After all, while buyers like seeing pretty pictures, they would also like to see who you are and what you are about before having you help them buy or sell a property. By watching and listening to you, they'll feel like they know you long before you actually meet. These videos can help you build your brand as well, as they give potential buyers a real feel for your personality.

Short-form virtual tours- These are typically short teaser videos. They mainly focus on the house's best features and are usually right around two minutes or less in length. Their purpose is to show just enough of the property to get a viewer interested in setting up an in-person showing or contacting you for more information.

In general, these videos don't require a long attention span, which makes them perfect for sharing on social media. They tend to work well on Facebook, Instagram, and other places where people are looking for interesting content to scroll through, but are not necessarily going for a deep-dive into a topic. In the grand scheme of things, these are great videos to grab someone's attention, but they don't generally *sell* the house.

Longer agent virtual tours/pre-recorded showings- These videos can be longer and go into more depth about the community, neighborhood, and features of a house or property. Agents make them to attract buyers who are serious about buying a property, as they are more likely to sit through longer videos. In addition to trying to sell the home virtually, these videos help agents begin building a relationship with an online audience.

These videos work best on platforms like YouTube, where they can turn up as a search result whenever someone Googles a specific address. They are also good candidates for Multiple Listing Services, which allow them under the assumption that people getting listings sent from the MLS are in the market to buy or sell a property.

NOTE: You can also take snippets from these tours and use them for shorter posts on Instagram and Facebook.

Lastly, these videos are great to have on hand when you get new prospective buyers or if you have an email list of people looking to buy. Basically, if someone is actively looking to buy in the range the house falls into, they're going to be willing to spend time watching a longer video.

PROS	CONS
• **Gets you in front of the buyer** • **Shows the seller you care** • **Allows you to highlight specific parts of the house/property** • **Can be done on your smartphone** • **You determine the timeline** • **You can shoot as much or as little as you need** • **Can have you featured in the video on MLS listings in most markets** • **Can save you hundreds of dollars in production fees that you would spend hiring a professional.**	• Takes more time on your end • You have to shoot and may need to edit the videos

Live Virtual Open Houses

Live virtual open houses allow you to interact with your audience. Much like a traditional open house, you will market it beforehand, get people excited, and then host them as you walk them through the property. Unlike other videos, virtual open houses allow potential buyers to request to go back to see something, inspect a feature more closely, or ask general questions about the neighborhood, yard, etc. This means they get to create their ideal open house with you via live communication. Not only are these live open houses fun, but they allow you to really build rapport with your potential clients.

The best platform for a live open house is Facebook Live, which allows you to have real-time conversations with potential buyers as you take them through the home. Since we are currently in a time where COVID put many places under "stay-at-home" orders, these live open houses have become more important. After all, right now, people don't necessarily want to risk going out, having conversations, and being in an unfamiliar home. Moreover, they may be ready to buy, but don't want to break their stay-at-home orders to come and see your property.

At the same time, sellers may not like the idea of strangers going through their house.

Like virtual agent tours, live virtual open houses are usually longer. This is to give you time to show the audience everything about the house and location, just as you would if you were hosting an open house in person.

NOTE: You can save these videos and, as with virtual agent tours, use snippets for shorter posts on Instagram and Facebook.

PROS	CONS
• **Allows you to take buyers' questions** • **Builds trust** • **Allows people to join who wouldn't be able to attend the open house otherwise** • **Creates a video you can reuse** • **The seller (and potential other sellers) can watch you in action** • **Custom experience for the audience**	• Requires a good internet connection • Requires multitasking • You only get one take • You have to watch out for the live comments

AGENT VIRTUAL/VIDEO TOUR VS. LIVE VIRTUAL OPEN HOUSE

Differences and Similarities

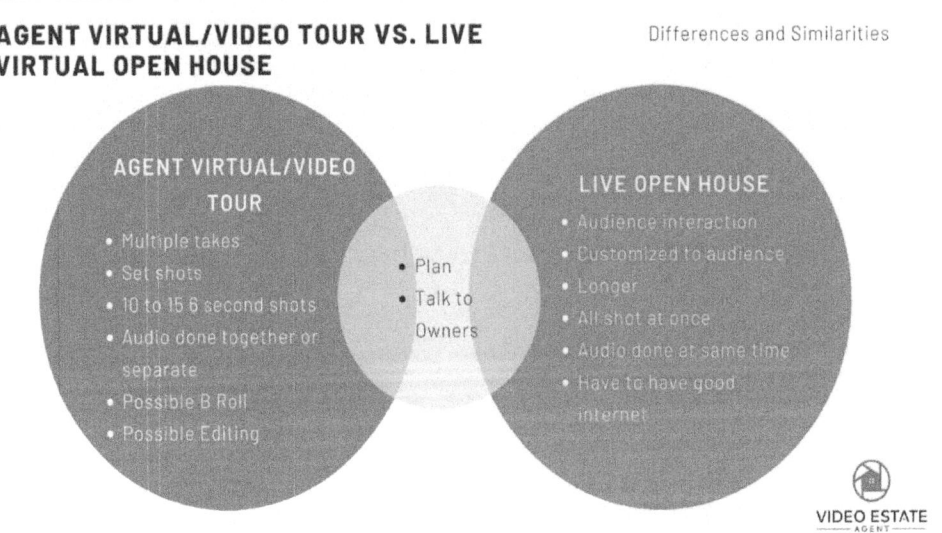

AGENT VIRTUAL/VIDEO TOUR
• Multiple takes
• Set shots
• 10 to 15 6 second shots
• Audio done together or separate
• Possible B Roll
• Possible Editing

• Plan
• Talk to Owners

LIVE OPEN HOUSE
• Audience interaction
• Customized to audience
• Longer
• All shot at once
• Audio done at same time
• Have to have good internet

VIDEO ESTATE
— AGENT —

Download this chart, and all other worksheets at
videoestateagent.com/virtual-tour-downloadables

Things to Consider When Choosing Your Type of Virtual Tour

When choosing the type of virtual tour you want to do, start by considering the sort of listing you have, the particulars of the real estate market in your area, and your goals as a real estate agent.

Type of Listing

While some properties fall into more than one category, most will fall into one of these six: high-end/luxury, mid-range, entry-level, investment, land, and specialty.

High-end/Luxury- The definition of high-end is dependent on the market you are in, but generally, they are the homes that are set apart by their price and location.

Mid-range- For the sake of this book, these are listings that are in between entry level and high-end. They tend to make up the bulk of the housing market in most areas.

Entry-level- These are lower-priced homes that typically appeal to first-time home buyers, singles, and people downsizing.

Investment- These are properties that people are buying with the intention of making a profit soon after. They include houses built on speculation (typically built by developers), houses that people are fixing up (foreclosures, estates, distressed properties, etc.), and rental properties (single-family or multi-family). Investment properties also include commercial properties for lease or sale (office space, storage, industrial buildings, etc.).

Vacant Land- Vacant land listings range dramatically depending on the area. Common land listings include: lots in housing developments, lake-front property, rural acreage, infill city lots, and land zoned for commercial use.

Specialty Properties- These are properties that are outside the norm for listings in your market, but aren't necessarily high-end. Some examples of specialty properties include homes on islands, log homes, and self-sustaining/autonomous homes.

Your Local Real Estate Market

All real estate markets are local and have standard expectations. In some areas, no one even does professional photography, let alone virtual tours. In other places, professional photography and virtual tours are expected with every listing. Only you know what the standard is in your area. Still, regardless of your market norms, doing an agent virtual tour is sure to set you apart from your competition and will help you attract new clients.

Your Goals as a Real Estate Agent

One of the questions we hear most often is, "Do you think I should do an agent virtual tour on every property I list?" Our answer is always that it depends on your goals.

For instance, if one of your goals is to set yourself apart from your competition with innovative marketing, then yes, you should definitely do an agent virtual tour. If you are a new agent looking to drum up business, then of course! After all, anyone with a pulse and a pocketbook will do!

However, if you are well-established agent, you may be able to afford to be more strategic and put your efforts into markets where you want to see your business grow. We will talk more about such strategies in the next chapter.

When to Use a Professional-Grade Virtual Tour

In most markets, sellers with high-end properties will expect professional photography and high-quality tours of their homes. Professional virtual tours are great in these cases, and we strongly suggest you use them as much as your budget allows.

When to Use an Agent Virtual Tour

Regardless of whether or not you have a professional video tour, we strongly suggest you create your own agent-led virtual tour as well. These tours help set you apart from your competitors and keep the focus on making a connection with potential buyers and sellers. Not only can you use these tours to sell your listings, but you also use them to sell *you*.

When to Use a Live Virtual Open House

Live virtual open houses are a great way to bring attention to you and your listing while giving you an opportunity to interact with people. While there are some challenges to overcome and things to consider before going live, remember that you can reuse the video footage to help give yourself a big boost in viewers. As long as you and your sellers are comfortable with live video, we suggest using it on all of your listings.

However, before hosting a live open, consider the following:

- Are you comfortable shooting video? If not, start shooting virtual tours until you are ready to take the next step.
- Do you have a microphone you can use? If not, live video is **not** a good option because it's important that your audience be able to hear you clearly.
- Does the house have a strong internet connection? Or do you have a strong cell signal at the house? If not, then live video is **not** going to be an option for that location.
- Do you want to engage with your audience and answer questions? Do you feel comfortable multitasking? If the answer is yes, then **live video** is the best option.

Listing Type	Professional Virtual Tour/360/3D	Agent Virtual/Video Tour	Virtual Live Open Houses
High-end/ Luxury	Yes/Market and budget dependent	Yes	Yes, if comfortable
Mid-range	Market and budget dependent	Yes	Yes, if comfortable
Entry level	Maybe	Yes	Yes, if comfortable
Investment	Maybe	Yes	Yes, if comfortable
Vacant Land	No/drone footage	Yes	Yes, if comfortable
Specialty Property	Market and budget dependent	Yes	Yes, if comfortable

Only you can know what type of tour is best for you, your market, your sellers, and your listing. Of course, you might want to try all three strategies at some point – be it to test yourself or to see which strategies work for which listings. In this course, we will be covering both the agent-led virtual tour and live virtual open house. Both take planning, both are personable, and both allow you to use your smartphone at your convenience. This is a win-win for you, your sellers, and your potential buyers.

In Chapter 3, we will go over the step-by-step process for preparing a video tour.

Download the following worksheets at: videoestateagent.com/virtual-tour-downloadables.

CHAPTER 1 REVIEW

Type of Tours

- ●
- ●
- ●
- ●
- ●

The Type of Tour I'd be Most
Comfortable with is _____

My Biggest Obstacle will be

_____

I Can Get Past it By

_____

The Best Property for Me to Start with is

_____

**Upon Doing Research I Found in My
Market, THIS is the Normal**

_____
_____
_____
_____

My Goal with Tours is to

_____
_____
_____
_____

NOTE SHEET

Chapter 2

Business Strategy

If you are looking for more business or are a new agent just starting out, virtual tours and live virtual opens are a great way to attract clients. Whenever possible, you should use them the same way you would an in-person open house.

The riches are in the niches. You can use virtual tours and live virtual opens as a way to help establish your specific niche. For instance, what areas do you want to specialize in as a real estate agent? Do you want to list and sell homes in certain neighborhoods (frequently referred to as "farming"), at a specific price point, or in a particular category? If so, seek out those listings when it comes time to shoot and post.

Now, there are no rules stating that you are limited to doing tours only on *your* listings. So, if you don't currently have any listings, ask other agents if you can shoot tours and hold virtual opens on theirs. You can either do this solo (just be sure to credit the listing agent in your introduction and have them get permission from their seller) or have them join you and hold a joint open.

If you want buyers and sellers in certain categories, then be sure to focus your efforts in those areas. For instance, let's say that you are listing a new build and want to position yourself as an expert in new construction. You might want to start by doing a tour of one of your builder's houses while it is still under construction. With video, you can document their progress each week while enticing your audience to follow along.

If you don't have an active build going on, consider approaching a builder and offering your services for free, guaranteeing them exposure on your YouTube channel. You could also ask the builder to share your videos to their social media pages to help get more social traction and increase the chances of driving traffic to your services.

You might also consider approaching FSBOs and asking to do a virtual tour of their house. After all, most home sellers would be thrilled to have someone do a free video of their home! Not only will you have the video to post on your YouTube channel, but they will be sharing it all over their social media as well. And just think, if their home doesn't sell, who do you think they are most likely to list with?

In addition to focusing on certain neighborhoods, some ideas for niches you may want to consider specializing in include: investment properties, commercial real estate, lake homes/vacation homes, patio homes/townhomes, condos, luxury homes, historic homes, and new construction.

Download the following strategy worksheets at:
videoestateagent.com/virtual-tour-downloadables

MY BUSINESS STRATEGY

My Current Expertise is:

I Want to be Known as:

My Target Audience is:

I Can Expand My Expertise By:

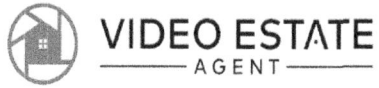 VIDEO ESTATE AGENT

NOTE SHEET

Chapter 3

Equipment and Lighting

A small investment in the right tools and a little knowledge of the basics of content, light, and audio will set the stage for high-quality video production.

The thought of producing, starring in, and editing your own video might feel incredibly intimidating. But, with some basic instructions and thoughtful planning, you'll be surprised how quickly you can make the leap, regardless of your experience with video. In fact, **all you really need to get started is your iPhone/smartphone** (we recommend an iPhone 8 or newer or a Samsung Galaxy 9 or newer).

For some of you, your smartphone may be the only piece of equipment you will ever choose to use. There's no need to purchase expensive equipment, nor is it necessary to hire an entire production crew. We're going to teach you how to use as little equipment as possible to get the very best video quality. With that said, a small investment in some additional equipment can go a long way.

Now, you'll probably be surprised at how little equipment it takes to make a professional-looking, engaging video. All you really need is:
- Audio
- Lighting
- Stabilization (we strongly recommend for taking virtual tours)
- Smartphone

For step-by-step instructions on how to use each of these pieces of equipment effectively, join our course at courses.videoestateagent.com/courses/virtual-tour-basics

Audio

Nobody wants to listen to a video with terrible sound quality, as they can be as unpleasant as they are hard to follow. That's why audio is one of the first areas in which video creators encourage newcomers to invest their money. For instance, you would be shocked at the difference even a $5 plug-in lapel microphone can make in your video's sound.

Now, our smartphones are designed to pick up sound from all directions. So, when you're in an open room, it will collect sound from all over that space. For instance, let's say you're in the middle of a 10'x14' room, and your phone is three feet in front of you. As you speak, your phone will have no problem picking up the words. The issue is that the sound of your voice will also bounce off of all of the walls. At the same time, your phone will also pick up whatever else is happening in the room. All of that sound can create a slight echo or "reverb" which can make the audio sound muddled or unclear.

Microphones, as opposed to phones, have much less "gain," or audio capturing signals. This allows them to pick up far less extraneous noise. So, in that same 10' by 14' room, a wireless lapel microphone (a microphone that attaches to your clothing and is attached to a lightweight battery or iPhone by an inconspicuous wire) can make a difference for a few reasons. The first is that it looks more professional and is far less distracting. The second is that it is designed to pick up on the sound directly above it (your voice). The third is that it allows you to walk around freely without worrying about wire plug-ins or sound quality.

Using these microphones with your smartphone is easy, as it features an adaptor that plugs into the same place as your phone's headphone jack. Once you connect it, your phone will then automatically recognize the new audio input and start waiting for sound to come through.

That said, you always want to double-check that your sound is being picked up without echoes or other interference. All you need to do this is take a few test videos and give them a listen. Of course, you may not be able to listen to your video with the microphone still plugged in, so if you don't hear any sound at first, unplug your microphone and play the video again. If you still don't have sound, double-check that both parts of your wireless microphone are on. Then, plug your microphone back in, and try again.

If you decide to shoot video outdoors, you'll get the best audio quality by adding a voice-over in post-production. This consists of shooting the video outdoors but recording dialogue inside in a room set up for quality sound capture. However, if you are going to be talking on camera while you're outdoors, you will have to use that audio (as your lips will be moving).

This means that if you do a voice-over, you'll have to match the words **exactly** to your lip movements. Ultimately, my best recommendation for recording outdoor dialogue is to wait until there is no wind, use the wireless microphone, and try not to move around too much. It's realistic to expect a little bit of noise when you record outside, but you definitely want to minimize it.

When shopping for microphones, look for what's called a **Lavalier mic.** Lavalier mics (otherwise known as lapel or body mics) clip-on or attach directly to a person speaking. They come in wireless, bluetooth, and wired designs.

Wired Microphone Setup

Wired microphones are very easy to set up. In most cases, you just plug the microphone right into your headphone jack. However, in some cases, you will have to use a lightning to 3.5 mm adapter. This is common if you have an iPhone and don't get a wired microphone specifically designed for that device. One end of the adapter will go into your iPhone, while you plug the microphone into the other end.

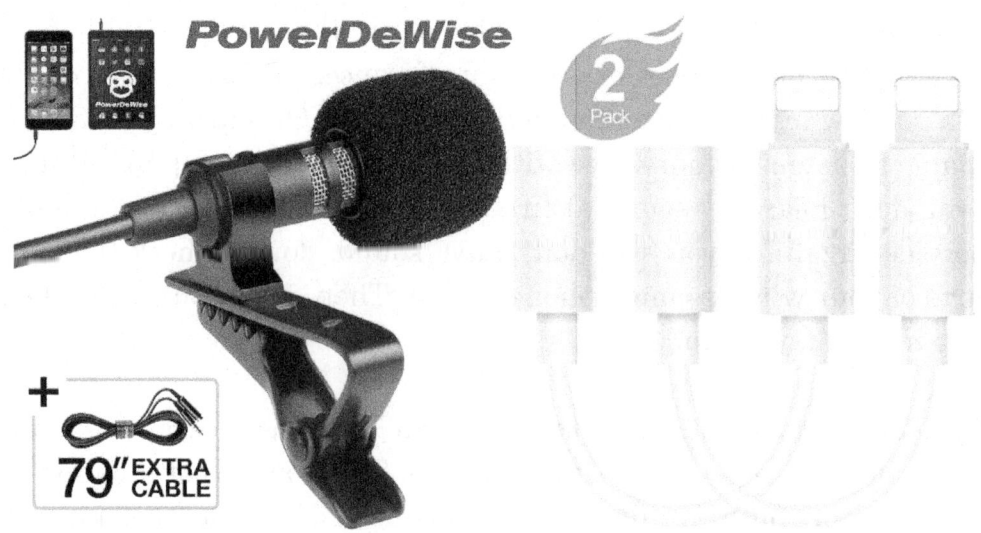

Wireless Microphone Setup

Wireless microphones are just a bit trickier, as they typically have more pieces. The first thing to look for is the microphone receiver. This is what will need to be plugged into your phone. Again, if you have an iPhone, you may need that lightning to 3.5mm adapter. Once you have the receiver plugged in, simply turn it on and move on to the next step. This involves setting up the transmitter, which is the small pack that you will need to carry in your pocket, clip to your belt, or carry in your hand. To get started, simply plug in your microphone and turn it on! After everything is operating properly, the two devices will connect to each other (you may have to sync them by pressing a button), and you will be good to go.

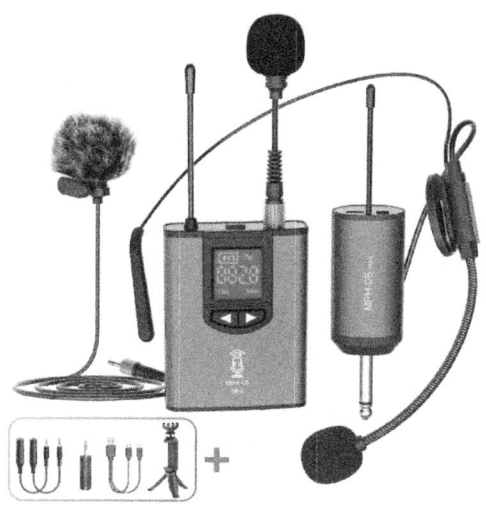

Lighting

Lighting is one of the key factors that will help make a video look professional. Of course, natural lighting is often best, and you should try to find a few places in the home that you feel will work best for your video. That said, there will be times where natural lighting is not an option or may not offer enough coverage to make a good-looking video. In these cases, you'll need to set up good **artificial lighting** to replace or supplement the space's natural light source.

Smart Tip: Purchase a 12" to 18" ring light mounted on a 5'to 6' tripod. This ring light will be perfect for either producing light or complimenting the available natural light.

Lighting Basics

You have already learned that the core of your business is selling *yourself.* A video may be the first time a potential client has ever seen you, so putting your face in the best possible light (pun intended!) is critical to making a great first impression.

First, ensure the lighting on your face is even and not too harsh or too dark. You can do this by putting your phone in selfie mode (where you can see yourself in the camera) and testing various places throughout the room. Below, we'll list the different types of lighting you'll encounter and the challenges they may pose.

Front Lighting

Front lighting is the best kind of lighting. While it may be hard to get used to, having light directly in your face (providing it isn't too bright) is the ideal way to film a video.

Back Lighting

If the light source is behind you, you might notice that you get an unnatural sort of "silhouette look." This is where the light is bright, but your face remains dark by comparison. A video filmed this way can make it hard for viewers to see your eyes, which will ultimately make it harder for them to connect with you.

- **The Fix-** If you find yourself in a position where the light is behind you, you have a few options to consider. The first is to simply reverse where you're standing and put the light in front of you instead. However, if you are trying to show off a large window or glass door and that light source *needs* to be in the shot, you can also try putting the ring light in front of you. This can help even out the light sources. The last option would be to turn sideways. This will allow you to talk about the feature while lighting half of your face naturally and lighting the other half using the ring light (on the opposite side of the feature).

Ceiling Lighting

Light from above can cast hard shadows on the bottom half of your face. However, the most common source of light in houses and offices often comes from fixtures placed on ceilings. This lighting is not very even, and for some, it can be very unflattering.

- **The Fix-** Again, a ring light should help with lighting from above. You'll want to start by placing the ring light directly in front of you to see if that helps. If not, you may need to lower your ring light in an attempt to even out the lighting. The main goal is not to get *perfectly even* lighting, but a clear shot without too much shadowing.

Side Lighting

Side lighting can happen when you stand in a room with a window or lamp on either side of you. Unfortunately, lights from the side can end up hiding half of your face, which is why they are used in gritty crime movies and film noir to set an ominous mood. Of course, that's the opposite of what you want to do in real estate! You want to use video to build *trust,* not give the impression that you're suspicious or untrustworthy.

- **The Fix-**There are a few things you can do to fix side lighting quickly. For instance, if you don't need the window open because it's not in the shot, pull the curtain over it to dim some of the light coming in. If a lamp needs to be on in order to show the room, try to move it in front of you. However, if either of these things cannot be changed, pull out your handy ring light and place it on the opposite side of your current light source (window or lamp). This will help balance the side light.

Attachable LED Lighting

Another tool that can come in handy is an attachable, battery-powered LED light. This light can attach to your tripod or gimbal (more on gimbals later) to ensure direct lighting in your shot. These devices are especially useful during videos where you're moving around rather quickly and won't have the time to set up and perfect the lighting for each shot.

Lighting is a skill that will take a bit of trial and error to get right. However, once you start to figure it out, it becomes second nature to make the appropriate adjustments. Ideally, you will learn to choose your shots based on the lighting, but there will be times when you have to work in a place with less than ideal lighting and have to find a way to make it work. It will only take a few of those instances for you to get the hang of using the tools you have to get the most of every shot.

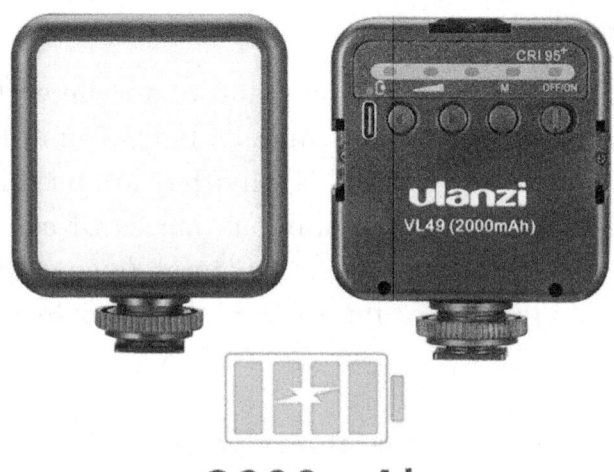

2000mAh

Ring Light Setup

Ring lights are set up much like tripods. You start by pulling the legs away from one another. You then open the clips, adjust the legs, and close the clips to lock the legs in place. The major difference is that you have a light that screws to the top of the tripod instead of a phone or camera. Most ring lights have an adapter that screws onto the tripod and the ring itself and a small ball that screws into it, which allows for adjustments.

If you plan on connecting your phone to your ring light instead of its own tripod, you will also need to attach your phone mount. To do that, you will need to take out the rubber in the middle (if you're attaching your phone to the bottom of the tripod) or put the rubber in the middle (if you're attaching it to the top of the tripod). Once you've done this, open up the mount, push the metal clasp over to lock it in place, and then push back the black clip (as if you were putting on a ski boot). Your mount should now be secure.

Lastly, plug in your ring light! Once you have electricity, you'll be able to hit the power button and use the adjustments on the cord to get the exact light you need.

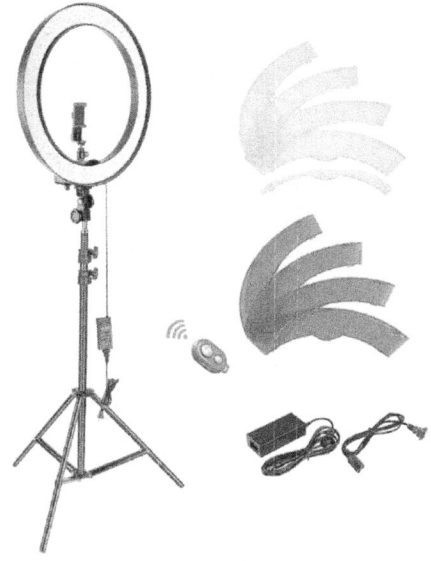

Stabilization

There are two main types of stabilization options: tripods and gimbals. A tripod is used when you are keeping your camera in one place. A gimbal, on the other hand, is best for stabilizing your camera while it's moving. Having both helps you include more types of videos during your tour.

Tripods

There are a variety of tripods and tripod-like gizmos out there these days. We suggest having an expandable 5 ft (or taller) tripod with a swivel head on it. This tripod will be able to handle most of the shots you'll want to take while *standing still*. For instance, if you want to get a left-to-right shot of the kitchen, you will be able to set your phone up on the tripod, and, using the swivel head, move the camera smoothly from left to right. Tripods are also nice to have when you want to take footage of yourself standing or sitting in one place.

Pro Tip - Most basic tripods come with a camera adapter on the head. You will need to purchase a phone clip adapter if you want to attach your phone to these tripods.

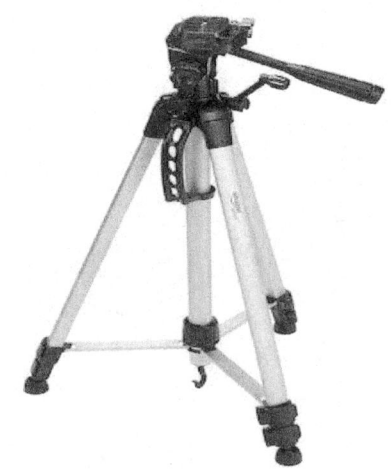

Tripod Setup

Your tripod will likely come fully retracted in a small box or bag. Begin the setup process by removing the product and pulling the three legs apart from one another. This will open up the tripod. Next, look for the small clips on each of the three legs. These allow you to adjust the height of the unit. After locating them, open up the clips and pull the legs down as far as you want them to go. Once they are at your desired height, close the clips again. Most tripods have three levels of clips and legs. Use them as needed to get to your desired height.

At the top of your tripod, there should be a screw sticking out. This is where you will screw your phone clip adapter.

Gimbals

A gimbal is a handheld, self-stabilizing, tripod-like gadget. There are many gimbals made for cell phones nowadays, and they all achieve the same purpose - making your videos less shaky! These devices are specifically beneficial in situations where you plan to be walking around during a virtual tour. If you've ever taken a video while walking, you'll notice the camera tends to jump up and down when you step. A gimbal can help you avoid this, which will make your videos look much more professional.

Pro Tip - We highly suggest getting a gimbal that also comes with a kickstand. This kickstand usually consists of three small legs that can attach to the bottom of your gimbal, allowing you to use it as a tripod as well.

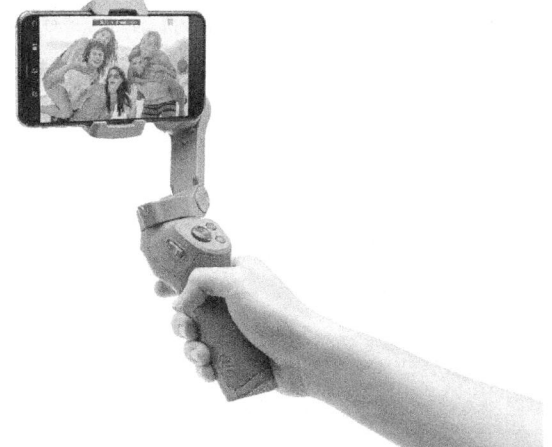

Gimbal Setup

If you purchase only one other piece of equipment, make it a gimbal. This will provide stabilization as you move about the house. Getting your gimbal set up doesn't take much time or effort. The largest consideration is making sure you've charged the device and that you have the coordinating app for your specific brand and model. Once your gimbal is charged, you may have to attach your phone clip (included with most gimbals) to the top of it. After you've done this, you can turn it on, then open the corresponding app on your phone. The gimbal will connect to the app via Bluetooth, and you will be ready to put your phone into the clip.

If you want to attach a light to your gimbal, you'll either need a **boot** that connects to the bottom of the device or a phone clip that has an extra adapter.

If you want to attach your **kickstand,** simply screw it into the bottom of your gimbal.

Smartphones

Thankfully, there isn't a ton you need to do to get your smartphone ready for shooting. Most modern smartphones have cameras that can easily compete with high-end, professional-grade cameras (especially if you're shooting in good light). While you don't necessarily need the latest smartphone model to shoot tours, it should be no older than three years, or it might not be compatible with some of the apps we'll be recommending.

The only thing you might want to consider to "enhance" the camera on your phone is a wide-angle lens. These lenses clip on to your phone and can instantly make rooms look larger. See the example below.

Regular lens

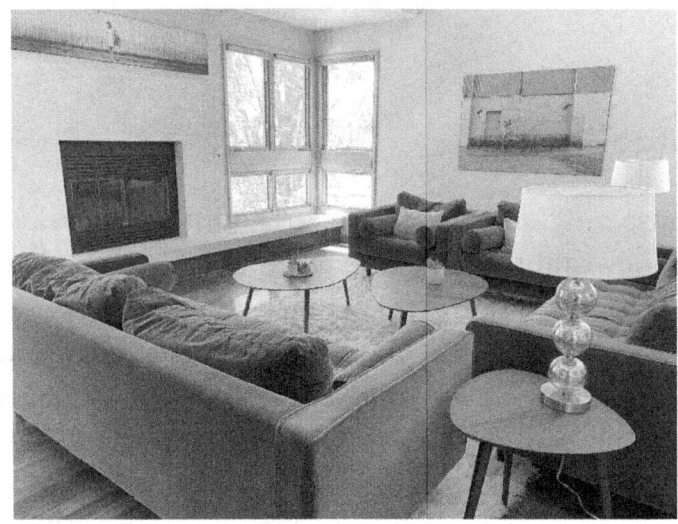

Wide angle lens

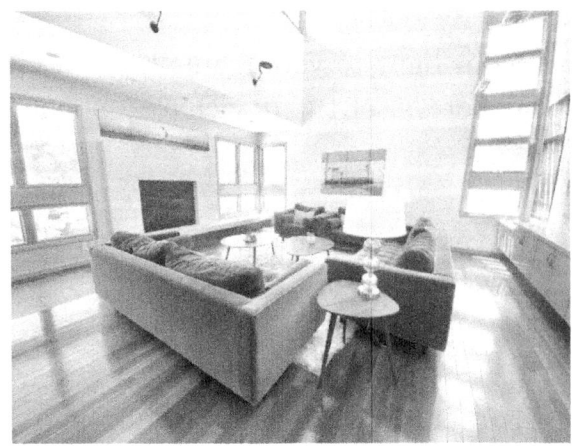

Note how much larger the room looks with the wide-angle lens? Again, this is not necessary for every shot or every house, but it is definitely a nice option to have.

Smartphone Setup

There are a few tips and tricks to consider when getting your phone ready for shooting. The first is to adjust your frame rate and resolution. The ideal resolution for your virtual tours (both agent and live) is **1080p.** However, we should note that not all platforms let you stream your live video at 1080p. This is fine - just choose the highest available.

You'll also want to set your frame rate to 60 frames per second. This will give you a fluid-looking video and allow you to slow down just about any shot you want when you edit the footage.

To set your resolution and frame rate, go to the settings on your phone and set the default to 1080p by 60fps. Alternatively, go into your camera app and click on the small number in the top right corner until it says 60. Then tap the letters until they say HD.

EQUIPMENT CHECKLIST

- [ ] Smartphone
- [ ] Phone charger cord
- [ ] Phone charger box/ adapter
- [ ] Tripod
- [ ] Phone mount for tripod
- [ ] Gimbal
- [ ] Gimbal kickstand
- [ ] Gimbal charger
- [ ] LED light attachment
- [ ] Ring light
- [ ] Ring light phone mount
- [ ] Extension cord
- [ ] Microphone wireless adapter
- [ ] Microphone pack
- [ ] Microphone charger
- [ ] Microphone to phone adapter
- [ ] MLS notes
- [ ] Planning worksheets or journal
- [ ] Pen

Test Your Gear

After you get all set up, be sure to TAKE PRACTICE SHOTS! You'll also want to take a few videos to make sure all of your equipment is working, specifically your sound.

Download the following worksheets at: videoestateagent.com/virtual-tour-downloadables

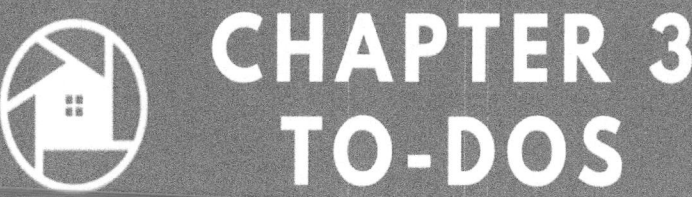

CHAPTER 3
TO-DOS

☐ Purchase all of the equipment you plan on using

☐ Set everything up

☐ Take practice videos

☐ Take practice audio

☐ Watch and listen to your practice footage and ensure everything is working

☐ Put together a bag where you can keep all of your video equipment

☐ Change your phone settings to 60 fps and HD video

☐ Try shooting in different lighting and correcting it with your ring light

NOTE SHEET

Chapter 4

Preparation and Video Content

Like all things in life, the more prepared you are, the smoother things tend to go. Video is no exception. When planning for an agent virtual tour or a live virtual open house, you and your sellers must work together. This small, but often overlooked rule is critical to hosting a successful video event.

As you and your seller prepare for the virtual tour, you want to be sure you discuss the content of the video. After all, you want to make sure you highlight the entire house, the property, the features, the layout - even the neighborhood. The more you cover about the house, the better for you, the seller, and the potential buyers. Let this be an opportunity to go over everything you would go over in an in-person tour. Remember, the quality of what you cover is just as important as how you cover it.

Step 1: Prep the Seller

Start with your sellers and have a discussion with them about what drew them to the house back when they first bought it. Was it the location? The large kitchen? What do *they* love about their house?

As a real estate agent, you may think the view from the living room window is the home's best feature, while the seller may think their bathroom light fixture (something you likely wouldn't have even mentioned) is the key to selling the house. Now, if you create a video and post it for the world to see without mentioning their bathroom light fixture, they are going to be very disappointed! Also, talk to the seller about their role in ensuring the house is ready for a virtual tour. In fact, we've created an extensive checklist for homeowners to help them prepare their house properly.

You can download all of our prep worksheets at
videoestateagent.com/virtual-tour-downloadables

41

VIRTUAL TOUR HOUSE PREP

EXTERIOR

- Make front entry welcoming
- Get rid of everything except the patio furniture and a few pieces of decor.
- All lawn equipment should be stored away in a shed or in the garage and kids' toys and pet supplies should be put away.
- Put away the lawn ornaments while the house is on the market and save those for your next home.
- Be sure to get rid of cobwebs, dead bugs, and general grime and debris from siding, eaves, porches, patios, decks, and outdoor lighting.
- Weed all planting areas and put down fresh mulching material.
- If you have outdoor pets, make sure waste is always cleaned up.
- Prune shrubs and trees. Keep plants from blocking any windows.
- Have your lawn freshly cut and edged.
- Make sure gutters are swept and cleaned.

GARAGE

- Sweep out and organize. Keep storage in garage neat and to a minimum. Remember, you want buyers to see that there is "room for more."
- Clean grease stains from garage floor.
- Remove cars from garage.

CLEANING

- Wipe down walls, windows, ceiling fixtures, air vents, switches and outlets, and doors.
- Wash curtains, floors, and rugs.
- Wipe, dust, or polish bookshelves, blinds, furniture, door knobs, and faux plants.
- Dust furnace and water heater.
- Wash the windows, inside and out and remove window screens.
- Clean ceiling fan blades and turn on ceiling fans at low speed during showings to demonstrate they work.

GENERAL DECLUTTERING

- Less is more - remove enough so that there is some empty space in closets, on shelves, and in cabinets.

- Put all laundry out of site, either put away or in hamper.

- Store portable heating or cooling appliances. (Don't give impression there's a problem with A/C or heating unit.)

- Put bills and other personal mail out of sight.

- Pack up personal, political, and religious items, including personal photos, trophies, collections, refrigerator magnets, etc. Potential buyers should not walk into "your" house; they should walk into "their" house.

- Clean up toys.

- Remove extra leaves from dining room or kitchen tables to make the room look bigger. Remove extra chairs from table if they crowd the table or fill up corners of the room.

- Clear off the dining table except for one nice centerpiece.

- Clear off all coffee tables and end tables in living room and family room. Keep decorative objects on the furniture restricted to groups of 1, 3, or 5 items.

- Remove any TVs, laundry baskets, and anything visible under the bed in all bedrooms.

- Make sure all beds are neatly and attractively made.

- Remove all visible storage boxes from basement, attic, closets, and garage.

- Take everything off closet floors.

- Put away laundry room soaps and supplies in cupboards and be sure laundry room counters and sink clean and empty.

- Keep all curtains and blinds open to let in all light and views.

- Turn on all lights and lamps for your virtual open house. Replace any burned out light bulbs with the highest allowable wattage light bulbs to brighten rooms, halogen bulbs are best wherever possible.

PETS

- Bring pets with you when you leave for your virtual open house!

- Keep any extra-loved pet toys and doggie bones hidden.

- Eliminate any food bowls, toys, or other signs of pets.

VIDEO ESTATE
AGENT

KITCHEN

- Make sure your kitchen is spotless. (Kitchens sell houses!)
- Remove or hide all small kitchen appliances and knife sets from countertops.
- Organize your pantry like a grocery store's shelves. Store or give away half the food in your pantry.
- Clean out your refrigerator.
- Clear refrigerator of magnets, pictures, messages, calendars etc.
- Wash all appliances inside and out.
- Wash and put away all dishes.
- Store all soaps, sponges and cleaning supplies out of sight under the sink.
- Remove all floor rugs to create more floor space.
- Clean tile grout.

BATHROOMS

- Remove all but the barest necessities in the vanity and tub itself, and put out fresh towels and rugs.
- Remove prescription medications from medicine cabinets.
- Remove personal necessity items from bathrooms, enclosed showers, and tub surrounds. This includes all shampoo, toothpaste, hairbrushes, dirty towels, etc.
- Dust furnace and water heater.
- Hide garbage can and store cleaning supplies out of sight.
- Keep toilet lids closed and toilet paper on the roll.

Define Boundaries

You also want to discuss areas that your sellers don't want to be shown in the video. In recent months, we've seen agents post videos of dirty garages, stuffed closets, and messy laundry rooms, and worse. Not only were we disgusted, but we simply couldn't imagine why they would do that to their sellers.

And while you can argue all day long that those areas should have been cleaned before they listed their house, we know that not every seller is in a position to have their house as show-ready as we'd like. Moreover, we know that imperfect homes sell **every single day**. So, while dirty, messy areas may exist, we certainly don't need to draw attention to them or record them in a video!

Taking the time to talk to your sellers and making a few notes will show them how much you care while dramatically increasing the chances that your video will be a success.

SELLER WORKSHEET

AREA HIGHLIGHTS:

WHAT DO YOU LIKE BEST ABOUT THE LOCATION?

WHAT IS YOUR FAVORITE ROOM IN THE HOUSE? WHY?

WHAT IS YOUR FAVORITE FEATURE IN THE HOUSE? WHY?

OTHER THAN WHAT YOU'VE LISTED, WHAT DO YOU WANT HIGHLIGHTED?

ARE THERE ANY AREAS OR TOPICS YOU DO <u>NOT</u> WANT SHOWN/DISCUSSED?

Step 2: Prep Yourself as Much as Possible

Now that you have prepared the seller for the virtual video tour, it's time to prepare yourself.

Show Up to Sell

Since this is your opportunity to show the house, you'll want to look and feel your best! After all, you only get one opportunity to make a first impression, so treat every virtual video like it's the first time someone meets you (because it very well could be). First, you should dress like it's an open house. Remember, your appearance is extremely important, as most clients tend to hire agents based on appearance and gut feeling. In short: look the part of a professional.

Know the Home

You should also prepare yourself ahead of time by doing a thorough read up on the house. Knowing the layout, the home's features, and all of the facts about the home will help you present it with both competence and confidence. This will also encourage buyers to trust your ability to help them find the perfect home.

When planning for a live virtual open house, make sure you have all of the key facts about the house fresh in your memory. For instance, you should be able to easily tell viewers what sort of foundation and heating system the house has. After all, you don't want to be on live video running up and down stairs searching for information that you should know.

Also, be sure to bring your MLS printout, feature sheet, or the downloadable checklist from this course so that you have all the info you need to answer questions. Perhaps an audience member will want to know if their furniture will fit in a bedroom. No one will expect you to know the dimensions of the room off-hand, but they will expect you to be able to find the answer quickly.

HOME FACTS

ADDRESS

LIST PRICE

BUILD YEAR

BUILDER

LOT SIZE

BEDS

BATHS

GARAGE

Stalls ____
Attached/Detached

FINISHED SQ FT

Square footage A/G_____ Square footage B/G_____

SIDING

Wood   Stucco   Brick/Stone
Shake   Cement Board   Metal
Vinyl   Engineered wood   Log
Other _____

ROOF

Metal   Tile
Asphalt   Rubber
Shake   Slate
Concrete   Other

FOUNDATION

Slab   ICF
Concrete block   Wood
Poured concrete

HOME FACTS

HEATING

Forced Air
Hot water baseboard
Dual fuel/off-peak
Radiant
Other_____

Steam
Boiler
Mini-split
Fireplace
In-floor

COOLING

Central   Geothermal
Window   Mini-split
Wall

SEWER

City   Drain Field
Private   Holding Tank
Mound   Other

WATER

Drilled Well   City
Sandpoint Well   Private
Other _____

DECK

Wood
Composite
Metal

UTILITIES COSTS & COMPANIES

Heat _____/ _____
Electric _____/ _____
Gas _____/ _____
Internet _____/ _____
Cable _____/ _____
Trash _____/ _____
HOA _____/ _____
Taxes _____/ _____
Insurance _____/ _____

ROOM SIZES

EATING AREA	KITCHEN

DINING ROOM	ENTRY

LIVING ROOM	LAUNDRY

MASTER BATH	MASTER

BATH #2	BED #2

BATH #3	BED #3

REC ROOM	BED #4

BONUS SPACE	BED #5

OTHER

Know the Location

One of the biggest mistakes we've seen agents make during their virtual open houses is failing to talk about the neighborhood or surroundings. I'll watch a video of them walking in the entryway and listen to them highlight the new tile, yet they don't say anything about the most important factor in real estate- the LOCATION!

Remember: location, location, location!

You need to highlight whatever you think might be appealing about the neighborhood or area to potential buyers. Some ideas might include:

- Convenient to shopping centers
- Close to parks
- Walking distance to schools
- Secluded and private

You may already have some of those details listed in the feature sheet or the MLS, but now you have the opportunity to give the information life and really sell it to your audience.

AREA HIGHLIGHTS

CITY:

NEIGHBORHOOD:

SCHOOLS:

PARKS/TRAILS:

STORES/RESTAURANTS

LOCAL ATTRACTIONS:

TRANSPORTATION:

FESTIVALS/EVENTS:

Step 3: Make a Plan

Be sure to plan the route you're going to take through the house and make a detailed list of talking points for every room. This is especially important when you are first getting started in videography. After all, when you are still new to the process, you may get distracted and forget key things you intended to highlight, including those features that are important to the sellers.

As Alexander Graham Bell said, "Before anything else, preparation is the key to success."

Choosing Your Shots

No matter what type of agent led virtual tour you are going for, you will have to have some idea of the shots you want to get.

For instance, if you are just looking to do a short-form video to get people interested in the home, you're going to want to film for around two minutes. In those two minutes, you really shouldn't show more than 15 - 20 shots. More than 20 shots will make the video too hard to follow and cause people to miss important information. Less than 15 shots will make the video boring and might cause some audience members to lose interest.

So, go through your room sheet and home facts and list the biggest selling points in order from most to least important. This will make it much easier to choose which shots to put in your short-form video while also ensuring that you don't take up a lot of your own time taking video you won't need. It will also shorten the editing process.

Something to note here is that a major selling point could be something simple like a kitchen counter. If this is the case, to really show off the kitchen counter, you will likely use a shot we call B-Roll. B-Roll consists of shots that help enhance the story of your video or your property. They're usually shorter shots that focus on something **very specific**. In the instance of a counter, you may take a closeup shot while walking down the side in order to really show the detail.

At the same time, many first-timers grab their smartphones and walk/talk through the entire house, ending up with a video that shows the same things three times, has their feet in it, etc. Viewers might also be forced to watch the agent climb the stairs and walk down the hall, causing them to get bored and click away. To avoid this, we're going to teach you how to have a plan that allows you to take long videos while still keeping things professional.

Of course, if you hope to shoot longer videos *without* editing, planning is going to be crucial. The last thing you want is to feel like you have to restart a video because you accidentally confused the utility closet with a walk-in linen closet, or you got turned around in the house.

We also strongly suggest you have a clear route that you plan to walk and stick to it. This route should hit on all of the rooms, features, and main selling points. Once you have your route, you will want to plan all of the things you want to catch on camera and find ways to avoid anything you don't want to show. For instance, in the bathroom, do you want to show yourself in the mirror? On the stairs, do you want to show the stairs themselves, the wall, or the guardrail?

Lastly, you're going to want to have talking points ready for each feature of the house as well as a few pieces of information to fall back on during transitions (like walking through a hallway). We also suggest noting these talking points on your route worksheet.

Always Take Note of:
- What needs to be in the video
- What shouldn't be in the video
- What is the most important to highlight
- How the lighting is for each shot
- How the audio is for each shot
- If there is anything you will need to change before you start taking your videos

Tips for making both agent virtual tours and for a doing live virtual open house:

- Be sure to talk to the seller first, get their input and permission to do a video
- Make sure the house is prepped correctly
- Make sure you know what shots you want to get in your video
- Make sure you are following all the NAR guidelines such as Fair Housing and Non-discrimination

To see a live coaching session on preparation, join our course at courses.videoestateagent.com/courses/virtual-tour-basics

The following guides are to help you plan your shots and tour route. They can be downloaded at: videoestateagent.com/virtual-tour-downloadables

SHOT LIST

Property Address _____

Shot Number	Room	Selling Point/ Focus	Shot Movement	Gear needed	Room Inspection Completed?
1					
2					
3					
4					
5					
6					
7					

My Tour Route

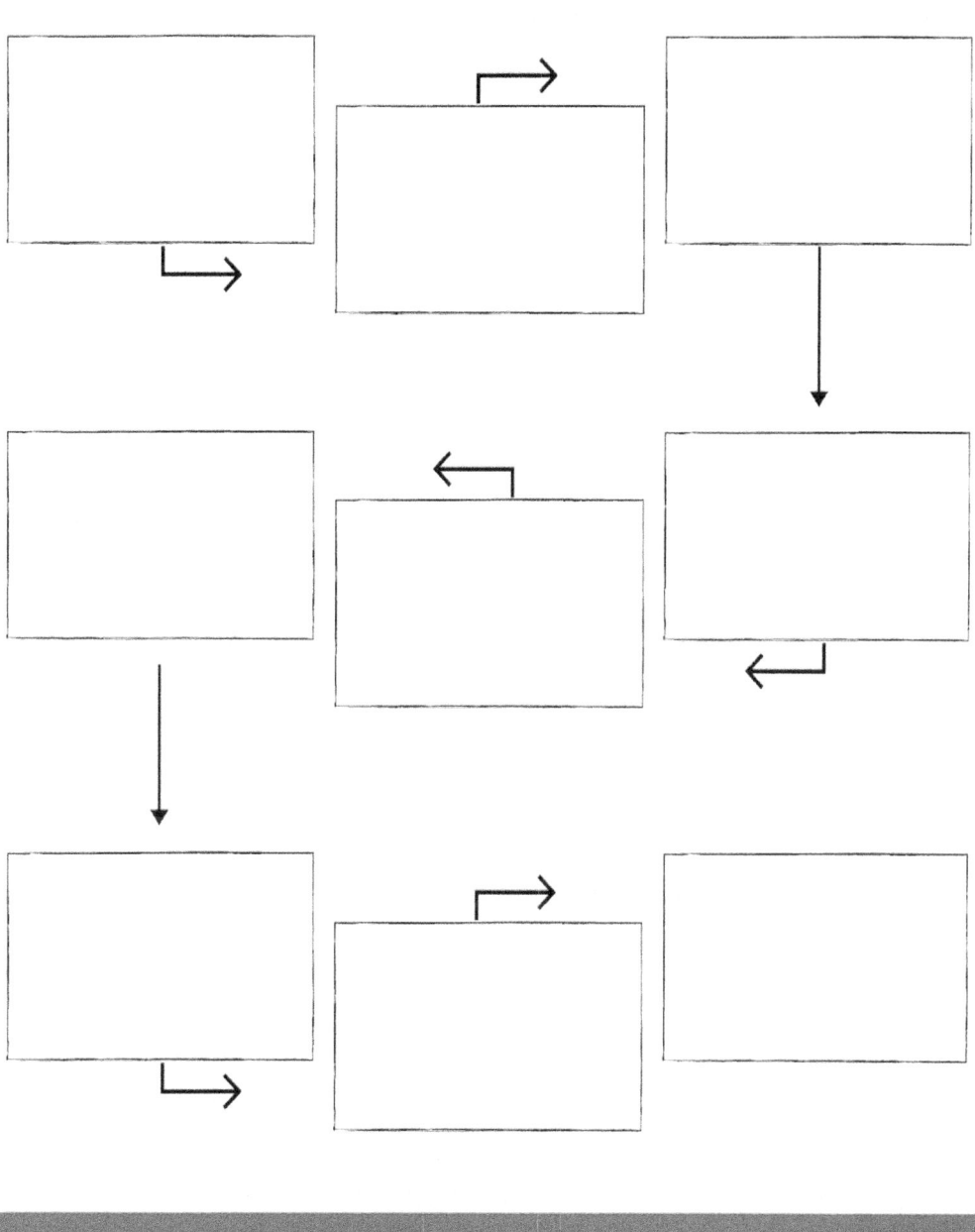

NOTE SHEET

Chapter 5

Hitting the Record Button

Lights, Camera, Action!

You have your equipment and are comfortable using it. Way to go! You've made some practice videos, you're prepared for the lighting throughout the house, you're ready for any outdoor shots, and you're all mic'd up. You also have notes of what you and the seller want to include and exclude in the video, and you know the house inside and out.

You are finally ready to start recording.

Most Common Shots in Edited Videos (Professional or Agent)

If you are going to be shooting an agent tour that you plan on editing or piecing together, there are only three shots you'll really need to know how to take.

- The pan shot: left to right or right to left
- The tilt shot: up to down or down to up
- B roll: start your angle back from an object and get close to it or vice versa

If you watch any Professional Tour, you'll notice that these are the most common shots used to show off a room as they add motion to an otherwise still frame.

Pan Shots

A pan shot is a relatively easy shot to take. Simply set up your tripod and place your phone on the top. You start by setting the camera frame all the way to the left or the right. Then press "record" and use the swivel to move the camera all the way to the opposite side.

Pan shots should be used when:
- You have a large space
- You want a space (or fixture) to look larger
- You don't have a wide-angle lens

Tilt Shots

A tilt shot is much like a pan shot. To take this shot, set the camera frame all the way to the top or all the way to the bottom of the room. Press the record button and use the swivel to tilt the camera all the way to the opposite bottom/top of the room.

Tilt shots should be used when:
- You want to show off ceiling fixtures
- You want to show off flooring
- There are tall ceilings
- There is a "big reveal" in the middle of the room (such as a gorgeous fireplace) that will catch the viewer's attention

B-Roll

B-roll is very different from both pan and tilt shots. Not only does it require different equipment, but it's used for a completely different reason. While pan and tilt shots are generally used to focus on an entire space or room, B-Roll is used primarily to focus in on a very specific feature - something that really tells the story of the property.

To take a B-Roll shot, set up your gimbal, put your phone inside, and get as close to (or far away from) the feature as possible. Press "record" and then slowly move closer to or away from the object

B-Roll should be used when:
- There is something unique about the house you'd like to highlight
- You want to add some excitement to your video
- There is a feature that really tells the story of the house
- You want to highlight selling points of the house

Voiceovers for Agent Tours

If you are shooting an agent tour, you will ideally be in the video at some point. During those times, you will want to make sure that you are mic'd up. After all, you'll want good audio for the video, and as we mentioned in the equipment chapter, microphones are the best way to get good audio.

If you are going to talk throughout your video, even when you aren't on camera, we do suggest doing a mic'd up voiceover while you're walking to reduce the need for editing. However, if you can't be mic'd up for some reason, you can always record a voiceover in post-production and add it to your video (see how to do this in the Editing chapters).

That said, it's important to have some talking points already planned out before starting your tour. These points can range from location details to home details to random facts. You can use this sheet to note specific points for each room.

Tour Plan Highlights & Talking Points

Exterior	Garage	Master
Entry	Mud/Laundry Room	Master Bath
Living Room	Storage	Bed(s)
Dining Room	Basement	Bath(s)
Kitchen	Outdoor Area	Other (recent updates, etc)

VIDEO ESTATE
AGENT

Shooting Live Video (and Unedited Videos)

Live video and unedited videos are special because you only get one shot at them. At the same time, taking these videos involves a very different process.

The House is the Star, but You Are the Host

When shooting a live open video, the focus should be on the house. However, you are the listing agent with whom people are going to be in contact. For that reason, you will need to find a balance between putting yourself and the home on display. So, while you don't necessarily need to be in every shot, you should be in about 30% of them. This is where the camera flip button comes in really handy. Don't be afraid to use it!

Control What You Can

When you are shooting a video that you only get to shoot once, you'll want to control every element you can! That means ensuring you have the house ready (lights on, doors unlocked, etc.), you have your route planned, you've eliminated any distracting sounds, and you have a well-lit place to sit/stand so you can talk to the camera.

How to Start a Live Video

To start your live video, you will want to open your Facebook app and navigate to your page. If you've created an event ahead of time (which you should have), you will then want to open that event. Once you're in, tap in the "create a post" box. One of the options will be to "Go Live."

Starting Your Live Video

When you start a live video, you will want to buy some time while everyone gets into the stream. A great place to do this is, surprisingly, in your car. Sitting in your car allows you to control your environment and can easily be played off as you show them what it would be like to walk out of their car and into their new home.

During this time, you'll want to be sure to greet people as they join the live chat, encourage them to engage in the comments, and introduce yourself as the listing agent.

Transparency During Video

Be honest and upfront during the video. People expect technical difficulties. After all nothing is always perfect when it's done live. So, be **transparent** with them. For instance, sometimes when entering certain parts of the home, the phone feed will cut out. You might want to address the issue BEFORE it happens by saying something like, "I am going to go into the basement now. I may lose reception here, or it may get a little laggy, but I promise I am coming back." Alternatively, you can get a Wi-Fi puck to boost the signal.

Another example includes when you're taking a longer agent led virtual tour, and all of a sudden, you remember there is something you want to show that you've already passed. If that happens, just be honest and say, "Oh, and I just remembered, there is something back here that you are going to LOVE!" That way the audience isn't confused as to why you are going back through the house.

Obviously, you can't control everything. You are only human. In fact, live videos are the most "human" videos you can watch- that's why they are so loved by audiences (snafus and all).

Remember, transparency earns trust, and trust is IMPORTANT.

Keeping Your Audience Engaged

Our number one recommendation for keeping your audience engaged is to *sllllloooowww down*! Take your time going through the house! Also, slow your speaking, as talking too fast can make people feel anxious. This is where planning comes into play. If you are prepared, you're not thinking too far ahead, which will naturally slow own your speech patterns.

Also keep in mind that it takes time to get used to walking around and talking on your phone. Practicing will help you learn how to do so naturally.

NOTE: During your videos, you will want to be reminding the audience that you are the listing agent and that they can contact you by calling or messaging you through Facebook. These are good ways to get your audience to try to engage with you *outside* of the video.

Be Conversational When Live

Don't leave your audience hanging! Make sure you are constantly prompting people to ask questions. You want them to engage throughout your live virtual open house for the following reasons:

- It helps you build relationships with the viewers. They see that you are knowledgeable and willing to help them
- It helps you show off the house by talking about it more
- You get to follow up with those people (because once they comment, you have their full name)
- It makes the live stream more fun and encourages people to stick around

A great time to take questions is at the end of your "tour." Ideally, you will have prepared a place with all of the home information written down. Once there, you can answer all of the questions from your "warmest" audience.

Tips for Shooting Any Video

For step-by-step instructions and demonstrations, join our course: courses.videoestateagent.com/courses/virtual-tour-basics

Know the Platform

Know which platform you will be using the video for before getting started. This is important because it will determine the length and the orientation of the video (horizontal vs vertical). For instance, Facebook and Twitter posts are horizontal, stories and TikToks are vertical, and

YouTube videos are horizontal. Generally speaking, as you can tell, most videos are horizontal. Thus if you aren't sure which platform you will be using when you shoot, it's safest to go with a **horizontal** orientation.

Don't Cut Off the Room

You want the room to look as big as possible. If you don't show the whole room, it can feel closed in or tight.

Tips for not cutting off the room:
- Use a wide-angle lens
- Set up the tripod in the corner of the room facing the light

Use Natural Light

Shoot during the "golden hour" (in the morning just after the sun rises or late in the afternoon as the sun is beginning to set). The natural light cast by the sun is best during these times and isn't as harsh as the direct light at midday. It is just this sort of soft, indirect light that creates long angular shadows, which often makes spaces appear bigger.

It is also the perfect light for filming because it won't overpower your room and will allow you to capture the view both inside and outside the windows. That said, different rooms might look better in a different light. For example, you might want warm, inviting light in the bedroom, while preferring to show the kitchen with bright, crisp light that showcases all its desirable features.

Don't Forget the Basics

Lastly, don't get overly focused on all of the technicalities the first few times you shoot. Just try to concentrate on getting the basics right.

Remember:
- Clean your lens before you shoot
- You can do your voice overs more than once
- B-roll is a good way to tell the story of the house

- If you're going to be moving, use your Gimbal

Take some practice shots of your own house while getting to know the video settings on your smartphone. Also, think of the listing you're going to be shooting. Do most of the windows face a certain direction? Will it be better to shoot in the morning or afternoon? All of these factors will directly affect the final result.

Download all of the worksheets at: videoestateagent.com/virtual-tour-downloadables

CHAPTER 5
TO-DOS

☐ Take a practice Pan Shot

☐ Take a practice Tilt Shot

☐ Take practice B Roll

☐ Take a practice tour of your house

☐ Try taking a video and talking at the same time

☐ Take a practice "live" on your personal Facebook or Insatgram

☐ Take a shot using your wide angle lens or setting

☐ Get used to walking around while taking video

NOTE SHEET

Section 2
EDITING

Chapter 6

Editing

Once you have your video(s) shot, it's time to make yourself look like a star! In fact, you'll soon learn how to take out all of the "uhs, hms, and ahs" fairly easily, as well as how to make your video more engaging, and brand-appropriate.

When we start discussing editing with most real estate agents, they get fidgety, give a little eye roll, get a disgusted look on their face and ask, "is this *really* necessary for me to learn?" In all honesty, *NO, it is NOT necessary for you to learn editing!* You can make great videos and never learn one thing about editing! In this next section we are going to go over the purpose and options in video editing and **teach you how NOT to edit.**

Option 1: No Editing

As a beginner, your unedited video will most likely contain "uhs and ms," some misspeaks, some dark spaces in rooms you are shooting, and some long pauses. You will also lack a proper "intro" and "outro" to your video and miss out on using added graphics. If you are okay with those things, you can go ahead and post your video the way it is. Just make sure you watch the video prior to posting (in case you overlooked a big blunder).

Now, while this option won't be for everyone, it can be viable for those who just need to get something out quickly. It's also fine for shorter videos that wouldn't need a lot of editing anyway.

Option 2: Hire a Teenager

This may sound silly, but trust me, if you know a teenager with a cell phone, they know how to edit videos! This can be a low cost (or even free) way to get some education on the subject (though you might have to deal with a bit of sarcasm).

Option 3: Hire an Editor

If you are a busy agent or simply despise the idea of learning anything in the tech world, then simply hire an editor! You can find one on Fiverr.com for as little as $5.00 (hence the name). This will ensure that everything is perfect, without you having to get your "hands dirty."

If you aren't familiar with Fiverr.com, it is an online platform that connects freelancers with businesses/individuals in need of their services. People from all over the world post their profiles and various services, so you can choose someone based on their country of origin, their skill level, timelines, reviews, and pricing. Still, keep in mind that some of the more economical freelancers are from overseas. This means that English is not their first language, so you need to be very specific with the directions you give them.

There are numerous other sites similar to Fiverr, such as Upwork.com, Peopleperhour.com, and Freelancer.com that you can also check out. We use online freelancers frequently and have had great experiences working with them.

Some of the services editors can provide for you include:

- video effects
- audio effects
- transitions
- video stabilizing
- trimming or cutting
- clipping
- color correction
- slow motion
- quick zoom
- volume enhancing
- reverse video

In order for an editor to properly do their job, you will need to provide them with detailed instructions. For instance, if you want a particular shot edited down, they will need to know the exact spot you want to make the cut. You can track that by looking at the time. For instance, you may want the "ummm" taken out at the 32-second mark.

Below, you'll find a helpful worksheet that you can use to better direct your editor.

Download editing worksheets at: videoestateagent.com/virtual-tour-downloadables

Editing Directions

VIDEO ESTATE
AGENT

THE TOPIC OF THIS VIDEO IS: _____

THE GOAL OF THIS VIDEO IS: _____

THINGS I'D LIKE TO SEE: _____
_____

TIME: _____ INSTRUCTIONS: _____
_____

TIME: _____ INSTRUCTIONS: _____
_____

TIME: _____ INSTRUCTIONS: _____
_____

TIME: _____ INSTRUCTIONS: _____
_____

TIME: _____ INSTRUCTIONS: _____
_____

TIME: _____ INSTRUCTIONS: _____
_____

TIME: _____ INSTRUCTIONS: _____
_____

TIME: _____ INSTRUCTIONS: _____
_____

TIME: _____ INSTRUCTIONS: _____
_____

Option 4 - Learn Some Basic Editing

A little editing in the right places can go a long way and it doesn't have to be too arduous. In this book and in our course, we teach you everything you need to know to get started in video editing. While there are loads of video editing apps and programs out there, we choose to work with InShot and WeVideo because they are just so easy to use. In the following chapters, you'll find step-by-step editing instructions for each of those programs.

That said, here are some basic actions you will need to know in order to successfully edit your own videos.

For step-by-step instructions, join our course
courses.videoestateagent.com/courses/editing-your-virtual-tours

Crop/Resize

There are going to be times when you want to adjust your videos. It could be to crop something unsightly out of a video, or it could just be because you want to use the video on a platform that doesn't support the original video size. Cropping and resizing allows you to change the video's overall size (think from rectangle to square, just like cropping a photo).

Trim

Sometimes the beginning or end of a video is a bit awkward. This could be because you were unsure if you were recording yet, you struggled to turn the video off, etc. This is where trimming comes into play. Trimming allows you to take off pieces either at the beginning or end of your video.

Split

If something happens in the middle of an agent virtual tour that you don't want to stay in, such as a misspeak, you can take just that piece out. To do this, we use splitting. Splitting will put a splice in the middle of the video and divide the video into two sections.

Delete

If you split a video with the intention of getting rid of something, you would split it on either side of that thing (let's say a misspeak). Then to get rid of it, you would simply delete it.

Mute

There will be times that you love a video, but hate the sound behind it. Muting your video, or turning the sound off permanently, will allow you to still use your video by eliminating unwanted noise.

Adding a Logo

The entire goal of using video is to get you and your brand in front of more people. That's why it is extremely important to brand your videos whenever possible. Adding a logo on your video is a great way to ensure your audience sees you and your brand in action.

If you can get these basics down, you will be able to do the editing on the majority of your videos. However, if you are looking to compete with more pro-quality videos or to be innovative with your agent tours, there are a few more functions that you'll need to understand. For instance:

Voiceovers

You can add your voice to a video *after* you've already taken it. This is called a voiceover. This is especially nice if you take a video or a section of video where you aren't on camera speaking that has a sound that you don't like. If you want, you can mute the video completely, then add a voiceover as a way to keep your audience engaged.

Tips on Voiceovers:
- Use an external microphone if possible
- Record in a quiet room
- Have a script prepared
- Try to record all at once (it's really hard to get the same sound more than once)
- Talk slowly

- Take test takes and listen to them before going all the way through your voiceover

Adding Text

If you really want to keep your audience engaged, we suggest sporadically adding text to your video. Some of the best ways to use text on your video are to show the address, share room sizes, or share an extra piece of information that you may have forgotten to mention.

Adjusting Lighting

This is where professional videos really stand out. In professional videos, you'll often notice that things look extra bright and white. This is done by adding highlights or getting rid of shadows in post-production using the editing platforms we will be teaching you.

Adjusting Speed

Keeping videos short and/or interesting can be a bit tough. So, a fun way to ensure you fit everything in is to speed certain parts up. For instance, if you want to speed up a boring walk up the stairs, you can do that. On the flip side, if there's a particularly breathtaking feature that you wish had more camera time, you could slow that part of the video down a bit.

Adding an Intro/Outro

A sort of bonus you can add to your video is to put a short clip at the beginning or end. These can serve different purposes. For instance, the intro at the beginning of your video may just be your name, photo, and the address of the house. The outro at the end, however, may feature your contact information or a call-to-action. These are great for engaging audiences and moving them from cold to sold.

BASIC EDITING GUIDELINES

Remember the rule of thirds

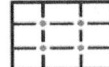

Things feel far more interesting if they are **not centered**. Always envision two horizontal lines and two vertical lines dividing the view into 9 equal boxes. The rule of thirds states that placing an object **where the gridlines intersect** is the best way to catch the eye.

Keep attention

Today's consumers are more distracted than ever, especially when browsing online. You have to **keep things interesting** right from the beginning. You have about 6 seconds to catch a users attention, and once they're hooked - to keep them hooked you want to continue to **introduce something new every 6 seconds**.

Uhs, ums, ahs, misspeaks

Everyone has something they do on video or when they give a speech that is **not the most appealing**. Whether you smack your lips, say um or make awkward pauses, editing will allow you to **take those moments out** and allow you to continue you to protray your best professional self.

Think of the flow

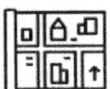

You want to consider the natural flow of a house when you are piecing together an agent-led virtual tour. You **don't want people to feel like they are being jerked around**. If you pan left to show one thing on a wall and pan right to who the thing next it it, it's going to feel weird! Try to keep things as consistent as possible (shot height, direction, light, etc)

Review your video

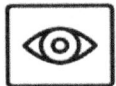

After you go thru and edit your entire video, you will want to **watch the whole thing back**. It may not be the most fun thing to do after messing with it for so long, but it imperative to **ensure everything looks and sounds the way you intended**.

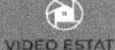

VIDEO ESTATE
AGENT

NOTE SHEET

Chapter 7

InShot

Many of us are on the go. Once we shoot something, we want to get it edited and out into the world as soon as possible!

InShot allows you to edit your videos right from your phone, is super easy to use, and is supported by both Apple and Android devices.

To get started with InShot, download the app at http://www.inshot.com/index.html

Get step-by-step instructions on how to use InShot in our course courses.videoestateagent.com/courses/editing-your-virtual-tours

Or, you can go to the app store and **download the app that looks like this:**

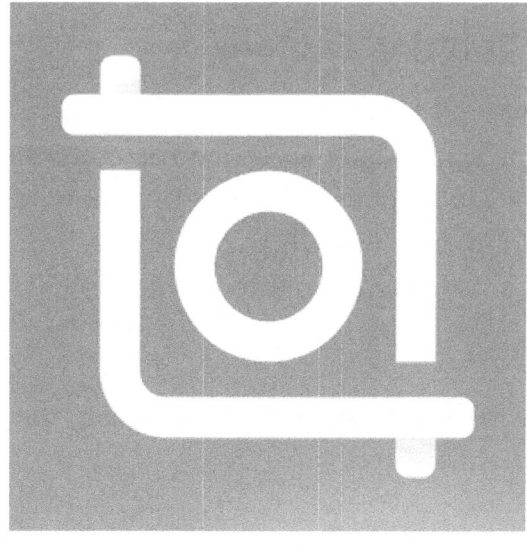

The Basics

Uploading Videos in InShot:

1. Open the app
2. Select "video"
3. Create a "new" project
4. Select the videos you want to edit
5. Select the check mark in the bottom right

Resizing Your Videos for Social Media

Make your videos ready for any platform:
1. Tap the clip you want to resize
2. Tap "canvas"
3. Select the size you want to use

Tap the checkmark on the right to apply to the selected clip or tap the checkmark on the left to apply to all clips.

If you want the video to fit differently in that size, you can crop it. To do that, select the clip you want to crop and use two fingers on the screen to pinch or pull out the video. This will make it larger (pulling out) or smaller (pinching in). You can then move the placement of the video by tapping and dragging the video.

Trimming and Splitting Footage

You can take unwanted footage out of your videos in InShot two ways:
1. Use the split icon, which will turn the clip into two clips
2. Tap the clip you want to trim. White bars will show up on either side of the clip. Tap the white bar on the side you want to trim and drag it towards the middle of the clip

Deleting Footage

To delete footage that you split, simply select the clip and tap the trashcan icon that shows up.

How to Mute the Sound of Your Video

If you don't need the sound in your videos for any reason, you can mute it quite easily.

Tap the video you want to mute, then **select the volume icon**. Moving the scale to the right will make it louder. Moving to the left will make it quieter.

You can apply this adjustment to the clip you have selected by tapping the single check mark on the right-hand side. To apply this change to all of your clips, tap the double check mark on the left-hand side.

Remember: Always watch the whole video to ensure everything looks and sounds cohesive.

Adding Your Logo

To add your logo to your video, you will have to bring it in as a sticker.

1. Get a transparent logo file (.PNG works best)
2. Save the file as a photo in your camera roll
3. In InShot, select the smiley face icon that says "sticker" under it
4. In the top menu, the second icon to the right will be a photo. Click it
5. Your camera roll will open, allowing you to select your logo file

Exporting Your Edited Video

When you're done with your video, tap the square with the arrow coming out of it in the top right-hand corner. The program doesn't actually edit your original file, but creates a new file in your photos. Once you exit, you will see that a new video will be put into your camera roll.

Advanced Techniques

Adding Voice Overs to Your Video

1. Tap the music icon
2. Tap "record." **The recording will start in 3 seconds!** So, don't tap "record" until you're ready

Note: If you add music tracks, be sure to double check and make sure they're royalty free.

Add Text to Your Videos

InShot also allows you to add text to your video if you'd like.
- You can customize the **color of your text** by selecting the color wheel and tapping "text"
- You can customize the **color of the line around your letters** by selecting the color wheel and tapping "border"
- You can customize the **box of color behind the text** by selecting the color wheel and tapping "label"
- You can also make the **text assets see-through** by selecting the color wheel and tapping "opacity"
- Lastly, you can change the **font** by selecting the "Aa" and scrolling through the fonts. Just tap the one you want to use

Adjusting the color of your videos

1. Tap the clip you want to adjust
2. Tap the "filter" icon
3. Tap "adjust"

From here, you can also adjust:

Lightness - Make your clips brighter by moving the slider to the right or darker by moving it to the left

Contrast - Make the difference between the light colors and the dark colors stronger by moving the slider to the right or less strong by moving it to the right

Warmth - Make the warm colors (red, orange, yellow) more intense by moving the slider to the right, or make the cool colors (blue, green, etc.) more intense by moving the slider to the left

Highlights - Make the light areas of your video lighter by moving the slider to the right, or darker by moving it to the left.

Shadows - Make the dark areas of your video darker by moving the slider to the left or make them lighter by moving it to the right

Slowing Down or Speeding up a Shot

If you want to change the speed of a video, simply tap it and select the speed icon.

From here, you can speed the video up by moving the scale to the left or slow it down by moving it to the left.

NOTE SHEET

Chapter 8

Getting Started with WeVideo

For heavier files, a lot of footage, or more complex projects - your computer may be the better place to edit your videos.

WeVideo is a paid, online video editing platform. In this course, we will walk you through making all of the necessary edits you need to on whatever computer you're using.

To get started, go to http://share.wevideo.com/W7BLn and create your account. You will get a 14-day free trial. After that, you'll need to set up your payments to continue using the program.

Get step-by-step instructions on how to use WeVideo in our course courses.videoestateagent.com/courses/editing-your-virtual-tours

The Basics

Importing your Videos Into WeVideo

Before working on WeVideo, you will need to upload your files from your camera or phone to your computer, Google Drive, or Dropbox account.

1. Login to your account
2. Start a new video project
3. In the "my media" folder, select "import"
4. Drag and drop your video files into the upload box. You can upload it from other sources by clicking on their icons in the left-hand corner, or by clicking "browse to select" to search your computer files
5. Select "open" and it will start importing those videos into WeVideo.

Remember: This does not edit your actual video file, but creates a brand new project for you to work on in WeVideo.

Once the pictures show up in the rectangles you will be able to drag and drop them onto your timeline.

Resizing and Cropping Your Videos

To resize your video, simply find the preview of your video. In the bottom right-hand corner, you will see one of three numbers: 16:9 (horizontal), 9:16 (vertical), or 1:1 (square). These are the only three sizes that WeVideo currently supports. You can change the size by clicking the number that is already there and selecting the number you want.

To crop your video, select the clip you'd like to crop. A line of icons should show up. Select the pencil. Doing so will open a new section on the left-hand side of your screen. One of the options in this section is "Scale." Here, you can change the zoom or crop by moving the slider left (to zoom out) or right (to zoom in). Once you've zoomed in or out, you can click and drag your mouse on the video and drag it where you want it.

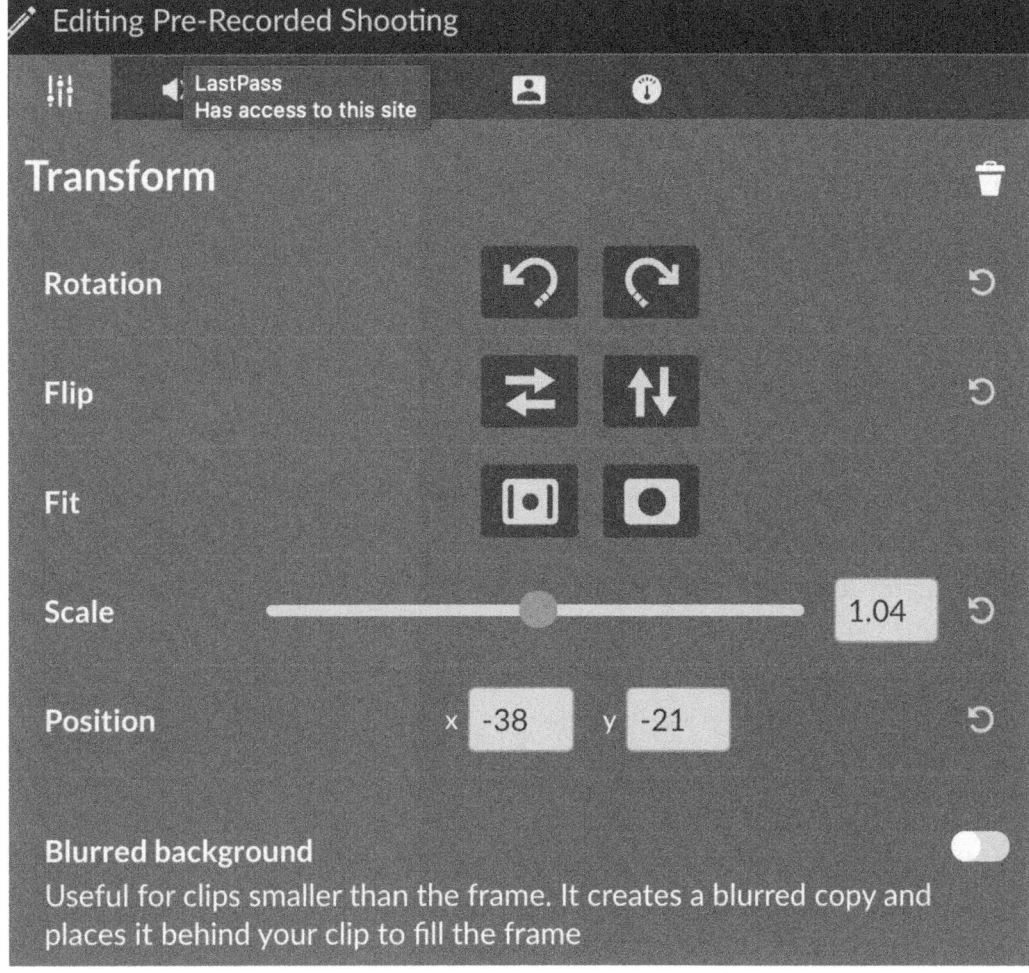

Trimming, Cutting, & Deleting

1. You can press the spacebar to start and stop your videos. This is the easiest way to navigate your video when splitting.
2. When you stop your video, there will be a blue box that shows up on the timeline. That box will have a pin and scissors in it.
3. Hit the scissors to split this clip into 2 separate clips.
4. Now you can select the clip that you don't want. If you hit the backspace button while it is selected, it will be deleted.

The other option we have for cutting is to grab the end of the clip in the timeline and pull into the middle. This will trim the clip.

Muting Your Video's Audio

With WeVideo, you can mute each clip individually. To do so, see the name of the clip and the volume bar on the left-hand side of the video timeline. Simply drag the volume icon to the left to make the volume quieter or to the right to make it louder.

Adding Your Logo

To add your logo, you will first need to ensure you have a transparent version of your logo saved on your computer.

When you upload your videos, you can also upload your logo by selecting the appropriate file. If you are adding in your file after you already started editing, simply select "import" from the top left corner. From here, you just need to select your image, and the program will import it into the project.

To put the image on top of your video, you will need to create a new video line. To do that, find the plus sign in the top left of the video timeline. Click it. When you click it, it will prompt you to select either "video" or "audio." Select video.

Once you have that new video line, drag it above all of the other videos you have. Then, drag the image into the new video line. Now, just position it on the screen wherever you want it.

Advanced Techniques

Adding Voice Overs

Voice overs are a great option if you don't have a microphone when you are shooting or if your video has too much extraneous noise. In this case, you can record your voiceover right into WeVideo. To do so, go to the same place you went to upload your videos. Then select "import" and "record."

Adding Text to Your Video

WeVideo allows you to add all sorts of text to your videos, including static, motion, and callout text blocks. If you're not sure which is best for you, you can toggle through the folders to check each option out.

Static - text that stays in one location as the video plays

Motion - text that moves into and out of the video as the video plays

Callouts - text that lays over a shape and stays in one place as the video plays

1. Go to the navigation bar at the top of the screen and press the "A" button. It will show you all the different ways you can add in text.
2. Go to STATIC and then to SAMPLE TEXT.
3. Grab this TEXT box and move it to where you want it.
4. View the text. If you don't like where it is, simply go to the PENCIL and change it

Adjusting the Color of Your Video

Many real estate videos feature a lot of color editing. This allows agents to create a number of different effects and make certain features stand out (while hiding others). In the WeVideo color adjustment view, you can easily adjust the following:

Brightness - Lighten up your video by dragging this selection to the right, or make it darker dragging it to the left

Contrast - Make your bright and dark colors more or less similar by moving this selection to the left or right

Saturation - Make your colors more intense by dragging this to the right or remove the color (eventually making the video black and white) by dragging it to the left

To adjust these things, select the clip you'd like to alter. In the blue box that appears above the video, select the pencil. The editing screen will show up on the left. In the top icon navigation, go to the circle half-moon shape. Here you can adjust the brightness (real estate videographers like high brightness), contrast, and saturation to your liking.

Slowing Down or Speeding Up Your Video

Moving the value from right to left slows the video down some. We shoot at 60 frames per second because it allows you to slow the video without losing the smoothness of the picture.

1. Select the clip you want to change the speed of
2. Select the pencil icon above the box
3. In the icon navigation, select the barometer
4. Move the slider to the left for a faster video or to the right for a slower video

Exporting Video

WeVideo has a somewhat odd export process.

When you are done with your video, you will **select the "finish"** button in the top right hand of the editor screen. From here, you get a few choices, but the most important thing to pay attention to is that you **always select HD.**

Now, to actually get the new file, you can either select the WeVideo icon or choose Google Drive, YouTube, etc. We suggest **just keeping it on the WeVideo** icon, as it is the easiest way to get your download.

Once the video is exported, you can **find it under the Exports tab** on WeVideo. There you can **select the downward arrow icon in the top navigation**. This will download the file to your computer.

1. Name your video, and press enter.
2. Once it is exported, make sure you watch it carefully. Remember, it can always be re-edited, as everything stays in your WeVideo projects.

NOTE SHEET

Chapter 9

Branding Videos

Branding is a huge part of the business world. People buy from the brands they know and trust, and familiarity helps people remember a brand, which lends to its credibility.

Branding ourselves as real estate agents is important. When we create videos, we want consumers to remember us and remember the brand we represent. One of the primary methods of increasing brand recognition is through the use of logos. That's why you need to make sure that your logo is on EVERY video you make. Not only is this a professional standard, it is a legal requirement in most states. It also allows people to see who you are, what agency you work with, and learn how to contact you. Think of the person who always wears a certain color or that radio jingle you remember when you hear the first note. People remember little things. You want them to remember you as well.

Using Canva to Create a Basic Intro:

Canva is a free service, but to get some of the animations we are going to talk about, you will have to have the PRO version. Luckily, this is well worth the money you'll end up spending.

Creating an Intro/Outro

An intro/outro is something you should import into all of your videos. Once the intro and outro are uploaded, simply place them at the beginning and end.

To create an intro and outro, we suggest using Canva.

1. Once you're in Canva go to "Presentation." This is important because this determines the size your regular landscape video is going to be in. If you are going to use this video for Instagram or Facebook, for instance, you can always go back and choose the preselected sizes from the templates.
2. Select the template that you like.
3. Put in your business name and customize as much as you want -- you can add shapes, icons, etc.
4. Double click on any of the text and change the fonts, colors, positioning, etc.
5. Upload your logo file by using the icon navigation on the right side and selecting "Uploads." Select your file and upload it.
6. Place your logo where you want it.
7. Once you have your graphic looking the way you want, it's time to animate!
8. Select the word "Animate" in the left corner next to the three circles.
9. Choose the animation you'd like to use.
10. Select "Download" in the top right corner and download the video an MP4.
11. Once it is downloaded, double click it and watch it. You can always re-edit it if you need to.

Using Canva to Create an "Contact Me" Outro:

1. Start with a presentation template again -- because there is usually a contact page at the end of these.
2. Find the "Contact Page" by clicking on "template" in the left-hand navigation and scrolling to the end of the page options.
3. Put in your business name and customize the template colors and fonts to your branding.
4. Upload your logo file by using the icon navigation on the right side and selecting "Uploads." Select your file and upload it.
5. Place your logo where you want it.
6. Change the template contact information to your information.
7. Once you have your graphic looking the way you want it, it's time to animate! Select the word "Animate" in the left corner next to the three circles.
8. Choose the animation you'd like to use.
9. Select "Download" in the top right corner and download the file as an MP4.
10. Once it is downloaded double click it and watch it. You can always re-edit.

Remember, you always want to encourage people to take the next step. These "contact me" outros are a great way to do that. Making these is quite similar to creating your intros, the only difference is the information you are putting on it.

NOTE: To find the links to your social pages, visit them and copy and paste the link from the URL address bar.

Adding Your Intro/Outro in InShot

There are two ways to do this:
1. You can add them using the plus sign next to the video timeline
2. You can add them when you initially pick videos to upload

Note: You must have the intro/outro saved to your phone in order to do this.

Adding Your Intro and Outro to Your Videos in WeVideo:

Now that you have both an intro and outro, we are going to bring them into WeVideo and start inserting them into all of our videos.
1. Go to MY MEDIA and select IMPORT. Here you will import your intro and outro either by dropping your media in or by hitting "browse" and selecting from your file folder.
2. Grab your intro and drag it where you want it on your video timeline
3. Do the same with your outro. Simply grab and drop it on your screen and it will play at the end of your video.

BONUS: Creating an Advanced Intro using Canva + WeVideo

To make our video a little more catchy, engaging, or advanced, we are going to bring it into WeVideo and add some music or recordings.

1. Select video just as if you are starting a new video again.
2. You should have already imported the video that you just created and now you are going to add music to it.
3. Go to the music tab by using the icon navigation and listen to a few to see if you like any of them. Try to find one that you think will inspire people to buy.
4. Select the one you like and drag it down to the audio row.
5. Trim it a lot (because you'll only have 4 seconds of video). This is fine, as you don't want your video to be too long. Now we have a nice video with music. However, it abruptly shuts off when it ends. To fix that, you are going to edit it just like you did your videos.

6. Hover over the box, click the sound button, and select FADE. Now we have an engaging intro that we can put at the beginning of all our videos.

7. Press finish, set the name and export it in HD. In exports, you are going to select it and download it.

This is now a whole new file, which you can upload into Inshot or WeVideo whenever you do a new video. Now you can put this at the beginning of your videos or right after the intro, when you may be speaking or showing a teaser of the house.

NOTE SHEET

Section 3

SOCIAL MEDIA STRATEGY

Chapter 10

Before a Live Virtual Open House

Making sure potential buyers know you are going to do a live virtual open house is important.

The more people know, the more likely they are to watch live or to watch when it is convenient for them. It is essential that you brand and promote these shows before you go live so that you can get as many people as possible to attend them. In this chapter, we help you develop useful social media strategies.

Facebook Events for Live Opens

Creating events for live videos is a great idea, as they automatically send out notifications if someone shows interest. For instance, if someone RSVPs as either "Interested" or "Going," they'll get a notification both the day before and an hour before the event happens.

However, we do suggest that you create your event 7-10 days before you host the open house. This will give you ample time to interact with your audience. Keep in mind that your event page is a great place to get people excited about the event and prompt them to reach out to you. Needless to say, having an event for your live open can be *extremely* beneficial.

For video tutorials on all things Facebook Events, join our course courses.videoestateagent.com/courses/virtual-tour-social-media-strategy

Step-by-Step Guide to Creating a Facebook Event
- Go to your Facebook Page
- On the top page navigation, select "events"

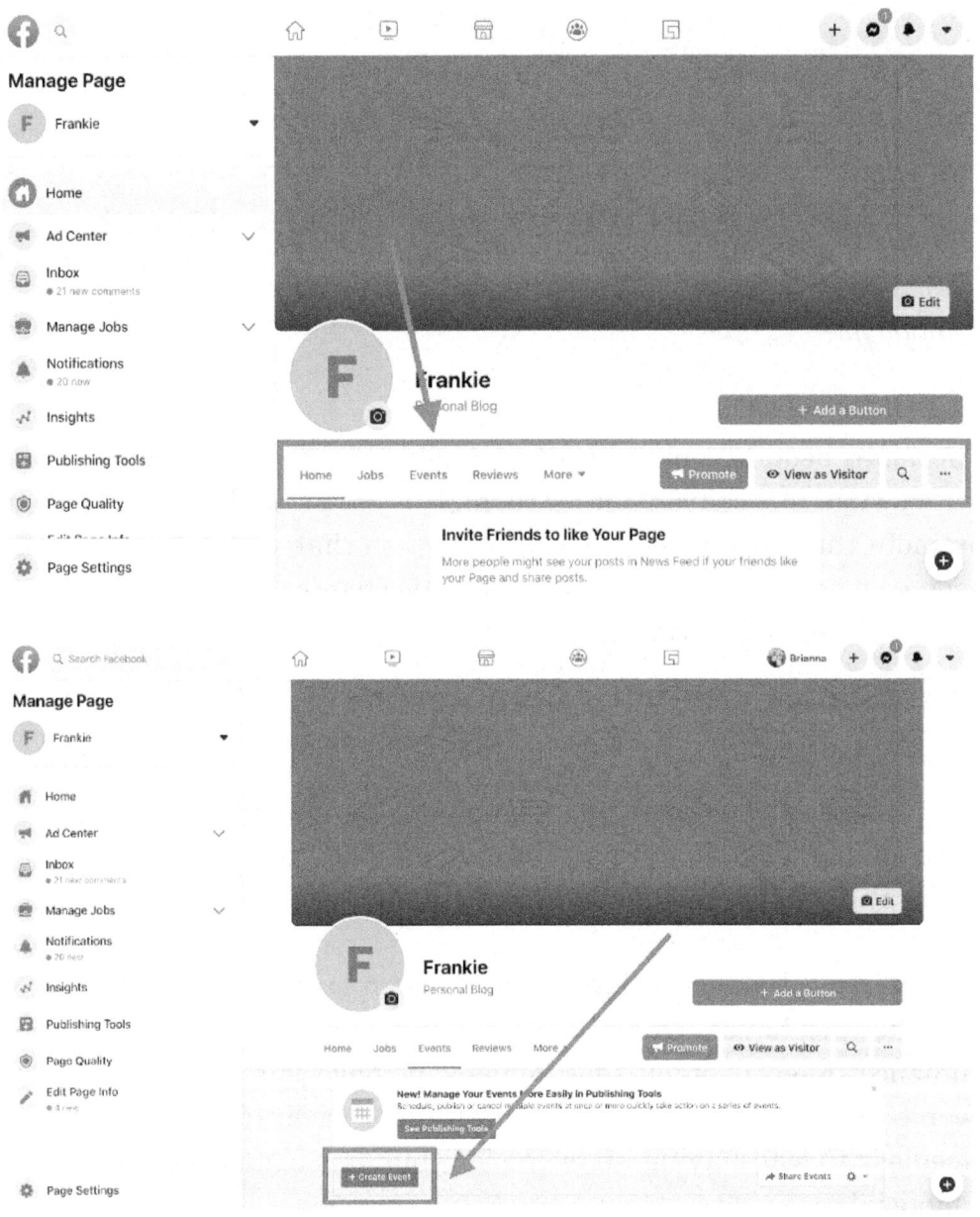

- Fill out all of the information you can
- Select "next" and "create" when you are done

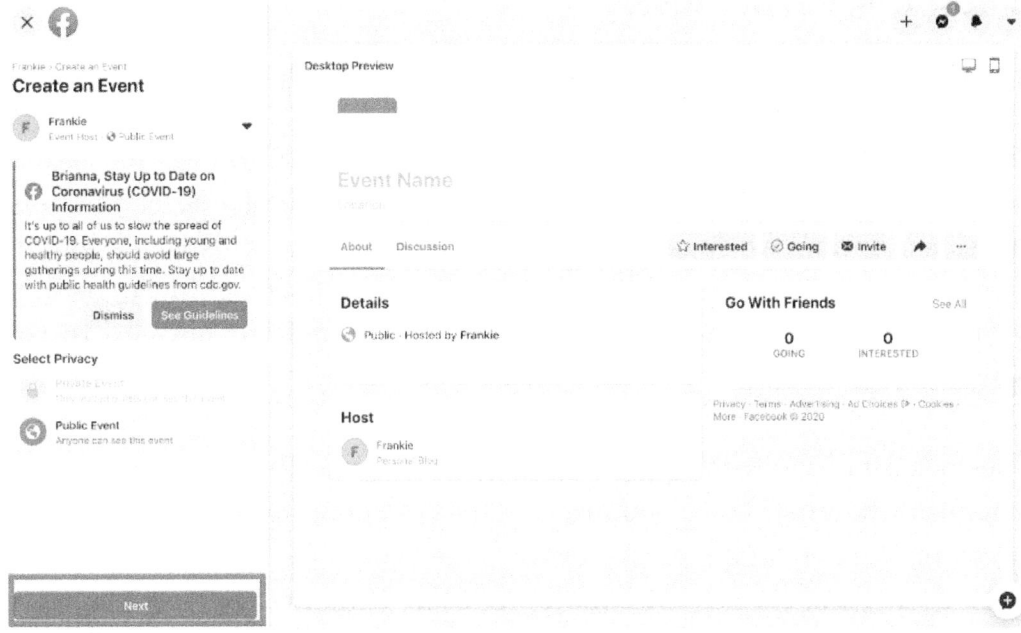

Now, here is the fun (more complicated) part. If you're not comfortable doing it, don't be afraid to reach out to someone a bit more techy for this!

- Copy the event URL from the top of your screen (where you type in things like "google.com")

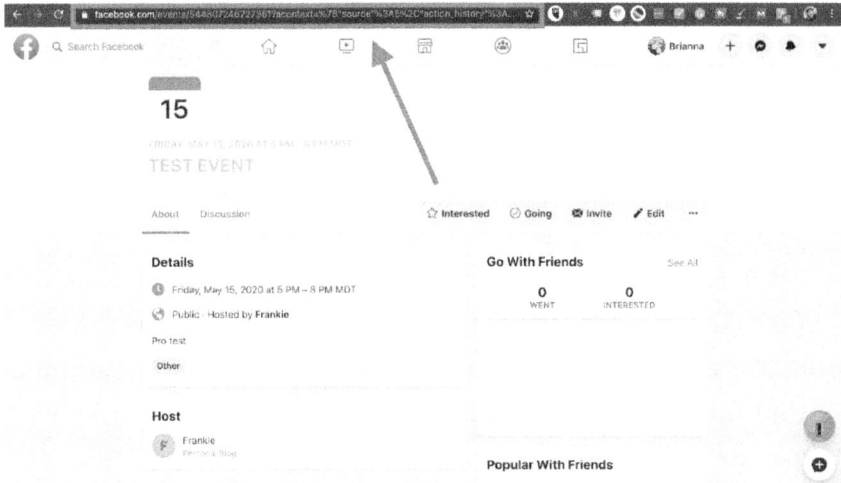

- Create a Facebook post on your Facebook Profile (personal) and paste the URL in your post

Facebook Event Musts

When you create this event, there are a few things you are going to want to remember. The first is that you should put "Virtual Live Open House" in the title as well as the property address. On the same screen where you fill out the title, you will also be able to add a description. In this description, we suggest letting people know that this is going to be an interactive experience during which you will be taking questions and requests. Also, be sure to remind people **not to show up to the physical the house.**

Besides all of the tech stuff, engaging in the event before you go live is an absolute must! Once you are seven days out from the live open, you need to start engaging on the event page every single day. In fact, this is a great time to ask the audience what they are looking for, have people post where they are from, or just try to get people excited about seeing the house.

Lastly, *incentivize people to attend.*

Did you ever do raffles at your traditional open houses? You can do them on your live virtual open houses too! Simply tell people to message you that they attended or send you a specific piece of contact information (so you know they attended AND you can get their contact information). If you plan on doing any sort of giveaway during the live stream, add this to the description too!

Sharing a Facebook Event

Be sure you share your Facebook event to your PERSONAL Facebook profile. After all, your friends and family are your biggest fans. The faster you can get engagement on your posts, the more excited Facebook is going to get - especially if you get comments. As engagement increases, Facebook will show it to more people because its algorithms focus on community conversation. So, ask people to comment in your post text! Be careful, though. You can't ask for comments in every post or Facebook will start flagging them. Be sure to save this tactic for really important situations (like live opens).

Who to Invite

You can invite all of your friends on social media, but you may have more luck targeting the people most likely to attend. For instance, if you live in North Carolina and are marketing a home on a golf course in your city, your dad's sister's brother-in-law from Arkansas is not as important to reach out to as the school secretary who knows everyone in your kid's school. And Suzie, the social director at the country club, needs to be on your "A list" to invite. You get the picture.

Also, don't forget about the people already in your network! Reaching out to buyers who have already expressed interest in buying is imperative. Ideally, you will either have their number to **call and remind** them of your upcoming events or, at the very least, have their email so you can include them in an **email blast.**

Invite your website visitors

Don't forget the people who come to your website! If people are browsing the houses you have listed on your site, you will want to encourage them to join you during your live open house. It's a great way to gain viewers and further engage with those people who might be interested in the listing. That's why we strongly suggest putting a link to any live virtual open houses on their respective listing pages.

Don't forget to email the people who are already on your list! You never know who is looking for a house (or who knows someone else who is looking). Word of mouth is a great way to get people to attend your live virtual opens – be sure to use it!

Post the time of your upcoming live

Don't forget to post the time of your live video event. You can post that you will do a live video at a certain time, which will actually put a countdown on the screen. This can be very helpful in getting people's attention. It would certainly get mine!

Here is an easy Facebook Live Event checklist for you to refer to:

Download this worksheet at: videoestateagent.com/virtual-tour-downloadables

FACEBOOK EVENT
CHECKLIST

EVENT INFO

- PUT THE WORD "LIVE" IN THE TITLE
- LIST THE ADDRESS IN THE DESCRIPTION
- PUT A DISCLAIMER NOT TO COME TO THE HOUSE IN THE DESCRIPTION
- USE A CUSTOM GRAPHIC

SHARING

- COPY THE URL OF THE EVENT
- GO TO YOUR PERSONAL PROFILE
- CREATE A POST
- PASTE THE LINK IN THE POST
- SHARE WITH YOUR FRIENDS!

STRATEGIC

- CREATE 7-10 DAYS IN ADVANCED
- POST DAILY IN EVENT TO ENGAGE AUDIENCE
- KEEP A LIST OF THE PEOPLE WHO RSVP AND/OR SHOW UP

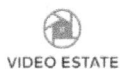

VIDEO ESTATE
AGENT

How to Assure Yourself (and Your Audience) that Everything is Working

We suggest doing a private live video before hosting one of these live opens. This means going through the entire process, creating a private event, and even having a few friends show up. This will help you be more confident when the time comes to actually go live.

On the day of your event, be sure to post a few times before going live. We suggest doing "countdown" style posts. Say things like, "just one hour until we go live at 123 ABC street - what are you excited to see?!" This lets the audience know they are in the right place.

NOTE: Always introduce anyone who is going to be working with you! You should introduce anyone who will be in the video with you, whether they are in front of the camera or behind a screen answering questions. Consider saying a little something about them, who they are, how they will be working with you, and why. You can also tag them in the video. This helps you network and gets the video out to their followers as well.

NOTE SHEET

Chapter 11

After a Live Open

In this section, we will help you understand how you can maximize the benefit of your live videos.

Follow-Up After the Video

Most of the time, the sell doesn't happen during the live video. This means you're still going to have to do some work.

Have a plan on how to follow up before you go on Live. This will help you make the most of the time you've spent with your audience.

If you want video how-tos for any of this content, join our course: courses.videoestateagent.com/courses/virtual-tour-social-media-strategy

View Your Post

You always want your Live open house to continue to remain on your Facebook page. To ensure it gets posted, always select "view post" when you end your video. Your post will be shown as your Live video along with all of the comments that came in during or after recording. From this screen, you have multiple functionalities that allow you to share your video with more people.

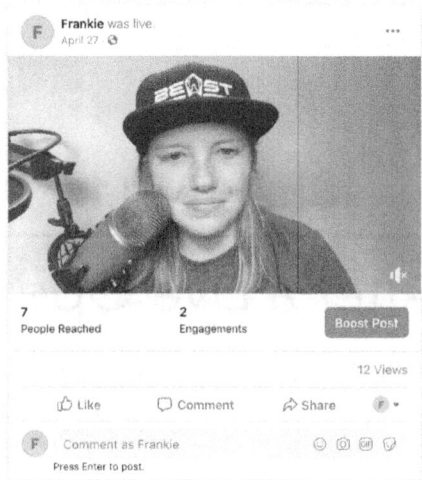

Thank Everyone

Obviously, you need to follow up and thank the people that attended and invite them to future open houses. If you can't message them directly on Facebook because you aren't friends, tag them in a post on the event page and say thank you (you can just make a list of these people and tag them all at once).

The ideal way to engage buyers after your live video is to reach out to them personally. If you did a giveaway, hopefully, you got some phone numbers or email addresses. If so, be sure to follow up with those people personally. If people commented on your video while you were live, be sure to go into the comments after the video is over, thank them for interacting, and give them your contact information.

Share Your Live Stream

At the end of your live event, Facebook will ask if you want to post the video....say YES. This is the beginning of the "follow up" process. As soon as your stream is over, you will be taken to the post that your live stream now lives on. From here, copy the URL in your address bar, and share it with any potential clients who may have missed the steam. You can send this link through Facebook message, text message, email - you name it!

Selecting the share button in the bottom right-hand corner also allows you to share the video to your Facebook friends, to any of your Facebook pages, or through Facebook messenger. You can even copy the link and share it with those who may not have Facebook.

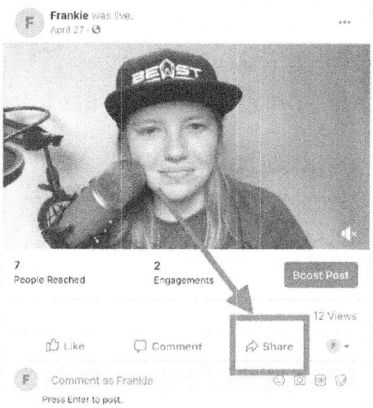

Own Your Video

After you go live on Facebook, make sure you SAVE and DOWNLOAD your video. To do that, go to your Live video post. From here, you can download it by tapping the three buttons in the top right corner and selecting "download." This gives you the raw video file that you can edit and upload to other platforms.

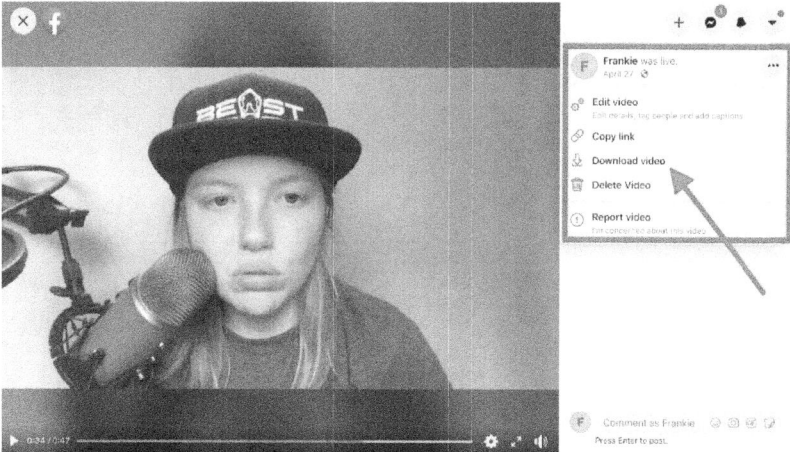

Use Your Videos

Downloading the video is also nice because then you can post it on any social platform afterward. This way, you have access to the video and other buyers who couldn't attend the live video open house (or perhaps "don't do Facebook").

You to edit it down into a few different versions:
- Long-form edited for YouTube (however long you want it to be, just take out the uhms, ahs, etc.)
- Short-form for Facebook, Email, and your website (about 2-5 minutes)
- Teaser/Preview for Facebook, Instagram, etc. (about 30 seconds)

Embed Your Live Open on Your Website

Now, fair warning - this may be one to hand over to IT or a web developer. But if you have access to your website content, you can actually embed your Facebook video onto your website by doing the following:

- Go to your Facebook Page
- Find your live post
- Click the "share" button
- Click "embed"
- Copy the line of code above your video
- Go to your website
- Get to the page you want your video to be on
- Paste that line of code

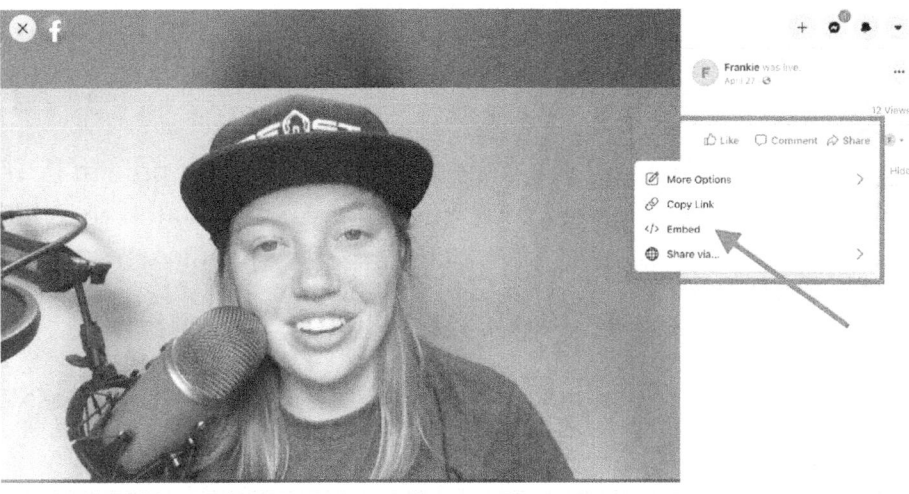

Embed Video

Copy and paste this code into your website.   Include full post

<iframe src="https://www.facebook.com/plugins/video.php?href=https%3A%2F%2Fwww.faceboo<

Advanced Settings

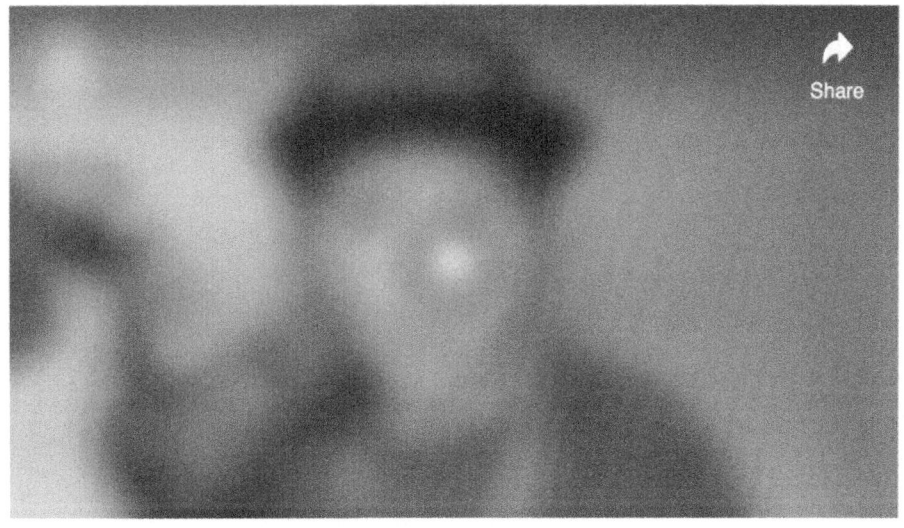

Serving Facebook Ads to People Who Watch Your Videos

In order to use "audience," you need to have over 100 people in it. If you didn't get 100 to RSVP or respond, but had over 100 watch the video at some point, you can get around this by targeting people who responded to your event!

Note: You may want to share this with your ad agency or marketing team.

Targeting people who responded to your event
1. Go to Facebook Ads Manager
2. Create a new campaign
3. In the "ad set"
4. Where it says "create new audience" see the line below it
5. Click the "create new" text on the right-hand side
6. From the dropdown select "custom audience"
7. From the screen, select "events"

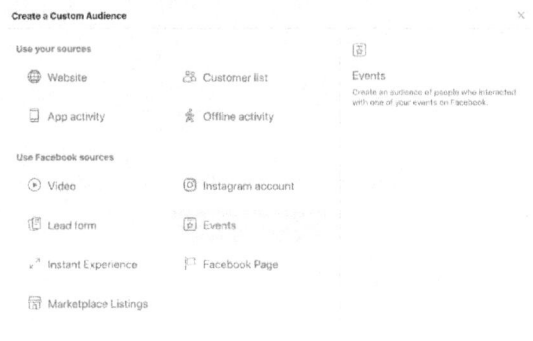

8. On the next screen, click "people who responded going or interested" to see all event engagement options and select the group you want to target

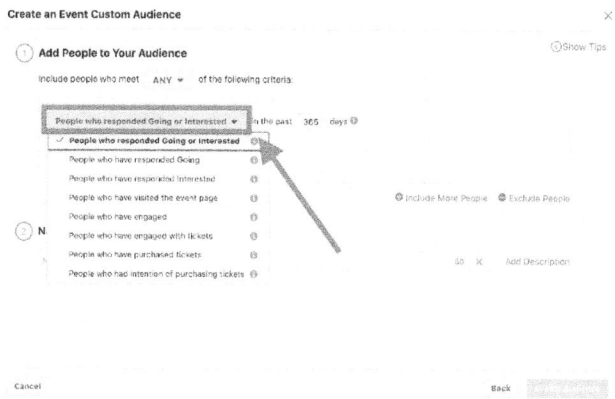

9. Then, ensure you have the correct "Page" selected and add the specific events you want to target the audience of by selecting "Select specific event(s)"

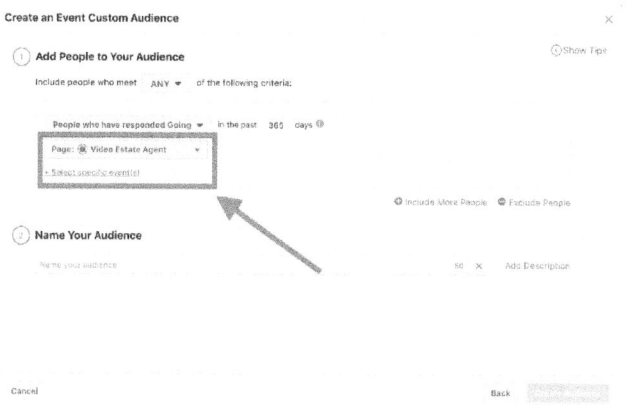

10. Name the audience
11. Select "create audience"

NOTE SHEET

Chapter 12

The Aftermath

You did it! You made your virtual tour or held a live virtual open house! So, now what? There are ways to continue engaging potential buyers with your saved videos, and this section is filled with tips on how to do just that.

You've put in your work. Now it's time to let the video do some work. For step-by-step instructions, consider joining our strategy course: courses.videoestateagent.com/courses/virtual-tour-social-media-strategy

Step 1: YouTube

We strongly suggest putting all of your videos, no matter what they are, on YouTube. This is because YouTube is the easiest place to store videos; you can navigate easily AND it's good for search engine optimization. Basically, when people are searching for houses, having your video on YouTube gives you the best chance of showing up in the search results.

How to Put Your Video on YouTube

Go to your YouTube channel. In the top left corner, there is an icon that looks like a video camera. Click it. You will be asked if you want to go live or upload a video. Select upload, then choose the file you want.

Best Practices

While your video is uploading, you will be given the option to fill out some information about the video - DO THIS! Here are some of the best practices to follow:
- Put the address (including city, state) in the title, as well as "For Sale" or your name
- Add a description that includes information about the house as well as all of your contact information
- Select a good thumbnail

- Create a playlist of "Houses for Sale" just for your virtual tours
- Always select that the video **is not** for kids
- Select "more options" and add relevant tags to your video (things like "houses for sale, houses for sale in Wichita, Kansas home for sale," etc.)
- Make your video public

Sharing Your Video with Interested Buyers

As we stated earlier, YouTube is the best place to store your videos as it makes for easy sharing. That said, once your video is on YouTube, you'll need to start sharing it with your clients right away. Sharing your video is as simple as copying the URL from the address bar on your YouTube video page and sending it to whomever you want. Much like Facebook, the link can be shared over a text, through an email, as a direct message, etc.

We will be going in-depth on how to get more views in the following sections.

Step 2: MLS

As of 2020, some videos you create will be eligible to be posted to your MLS listing. Now, it should be noted that this is very new territory. Previously, it was not possible to use your agent virtual tour videos at all. Even now, you can only do so in certain instances.

The current stipulations (in most places) state that videos *cannot be branded.* There is a lot of interpretation that goes into that statement. Branded could mean saying your name, saying your brokerage name - or it could even mean showing your face! However, we are seeing that more times than not, there is a good possibility that you can get away with actually being in the video talking as long as you **do not** introduce yourself. Now, this may seem weird (and it is), but it is the only way for you to get yourself in front of the audience and get them interested in you as a real estate agent.

Now, there are exceptions to this stipulation in some places. Moreover, some services will allow you to upload both a branded and unbranded video - **so always check your service's regulations.**

All of this being said, the day that you publish your video to YouTube, you will also want to post it to your MLS listing. To do that, you will just need your YouTube link. From there, just go into your MLS listing and drop the link wherever it asks for it. Make sure you check with your MLS provider, however. They may require you to use a different link.

Step 3: Email

Email is one of the best ways to reach out to potential buyers, as they have already shown that they trust you enough to give you their contact info.

Sharing your virtual tour via email is easy once you have it uploaded to YouTube. Depending on your email marketing platform, you will need either the URL of the video, or the embed code.

1. Select "share" at the bottom right corner of your video.

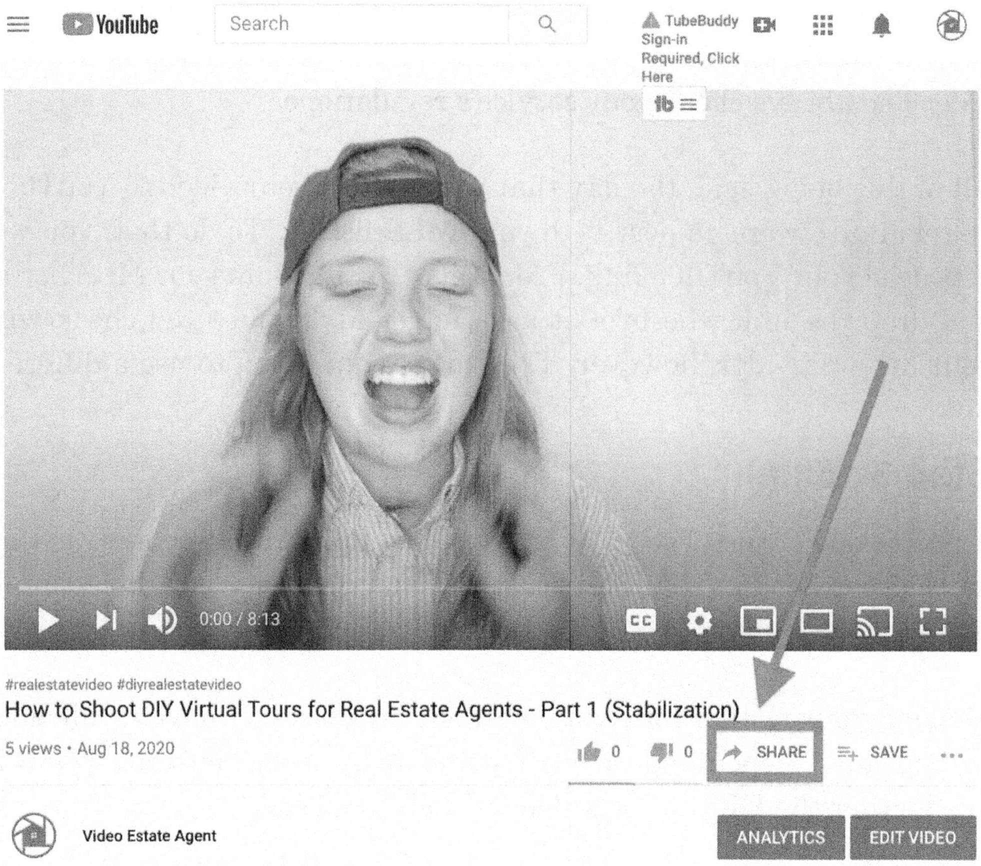

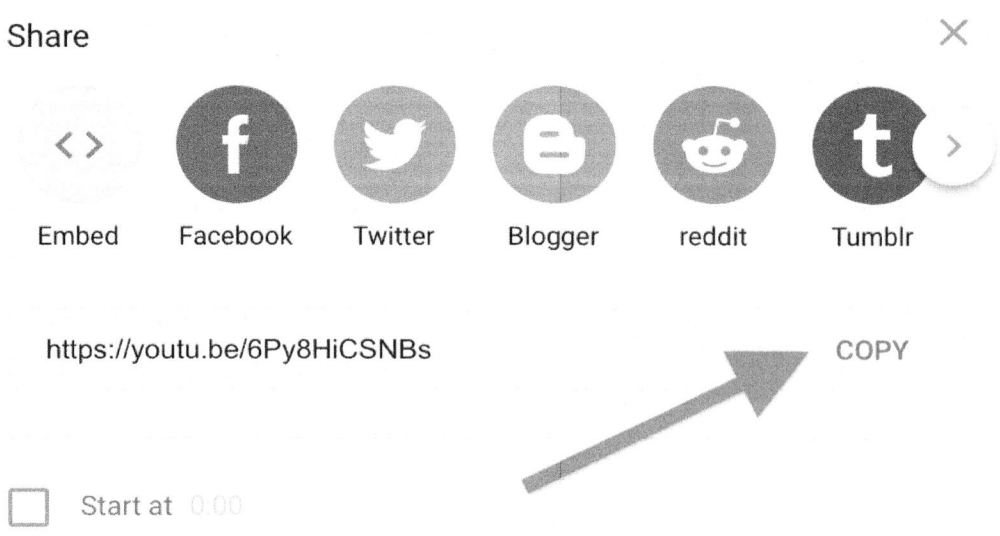

2.   This will show you the URL you need to share. To copy it, just select "copy".

136

3. If you need the embed code, simply select "Embed"

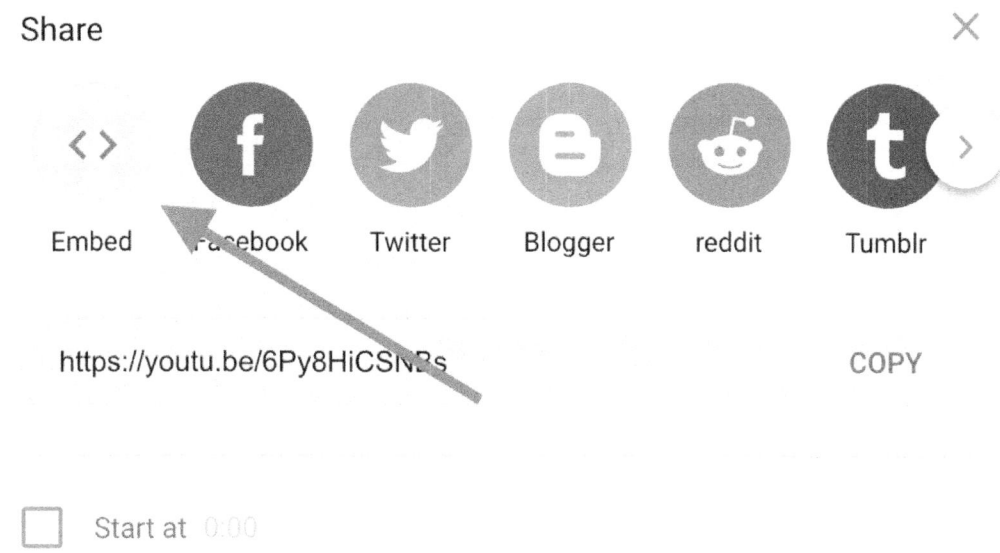

4. Copy the embed code given

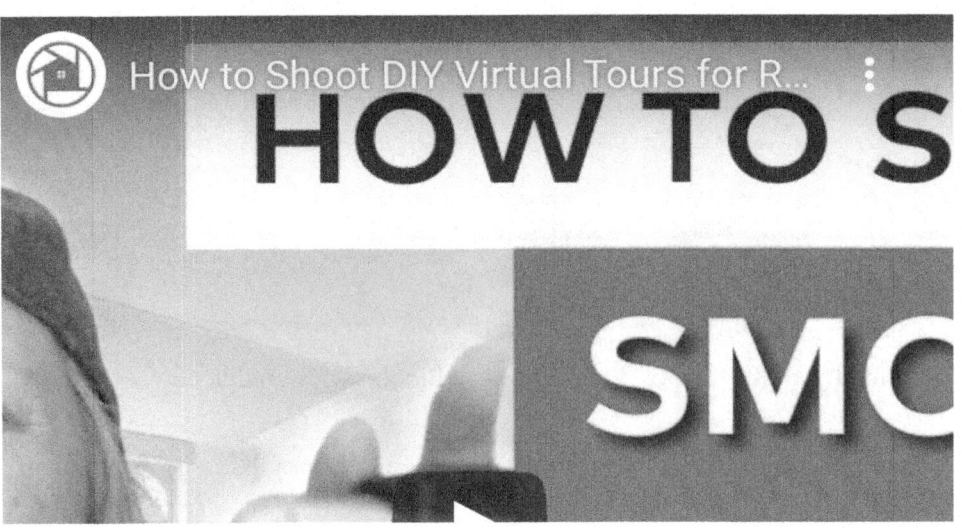

Embed Video ✕

```
<iframe width="560" height="315"
src="https://www.youtube.com/embed/6Py8H
iCSNBs" frameborder="0"
allow="accelerometer; autoplay;
encrypted-media; gyroscope; picture-in-
picture" allowfullscreen></iframe>
```

☐ Start at 0:00

EMBED OPTIONS

☑ Show player controls.

☐ Enable privacy-enhanced mode. ⓘ

COPY

Once you have what you need copied, you will need to draft up a quick email. If you have just a few people to share the house with, feel free to create personalized emails for each of those potential buyers. The email should include points that make the house particularly perfect for that client.

If you have a larger list of clients that you think may be interested in the house, or if you just want to share the email with as many people as possible, we suggest listing a few of the property's bigger selling points as well as the MLS information.

You might also consider sending the tour video out in a weekly newsletter if you have one. This is the perfect place to reach a large number of people who may be interested in buying or who know someone in the market for a home.

No matter what kind of email you send out, always be sure to prompt buyers to take the next step by either calling you or setting up a showing.

Step 4: Facebook

There are a few ways to put a video on Facebook. Obviously, you can just load the whole thing up like you would a photo. That said, if you have a video that's longer than two minutes, and you get in front of a bunch of people who aren't yet interested, you may lose their interest. That is why we suggest doing a "roll-out" of your virtual tours.

Virtual Tour Roll-Out

The hope is that you will put your agent virtual tour out and someone will watch the video all the way through, then call you to set up a showing or, even better, with an offer!

Day 1

To get people to this point, you first need to get them familiar with the house. So, the day after you post your video to YouTube, we suggest starting by posting something that will give people basic information about the house. These are the posts people are most used to seeing. Sometimes they are just a short highlight clip or even a few photos attached to some very standard info.

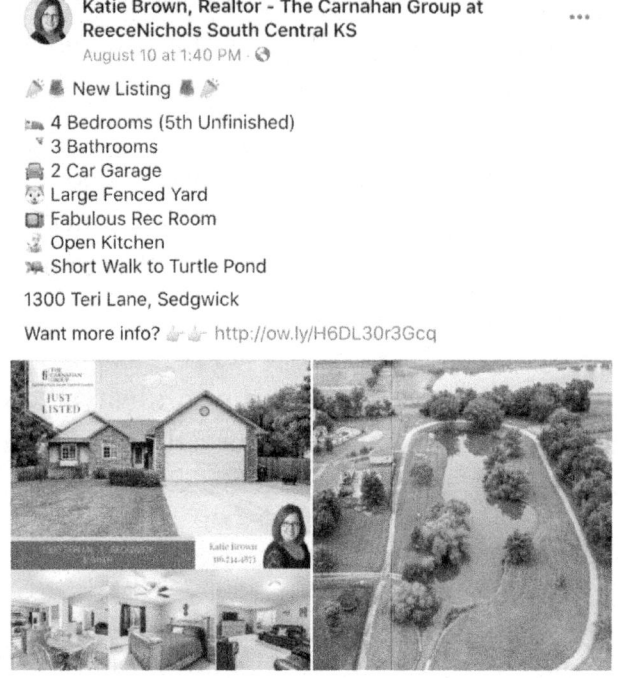

Now, we also suggest adding in a photo or line of text that lets people know a virtual tour of the home will be on your page soon. This gets the audience primed for engaged viewing!

Day 3/4

When you're ready to post the video (around 2-3 days later), we suggest posting the YouTube link. A video preview will auto-populate, allowing people to watch the video right from Facebook.

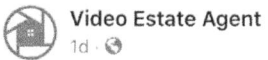

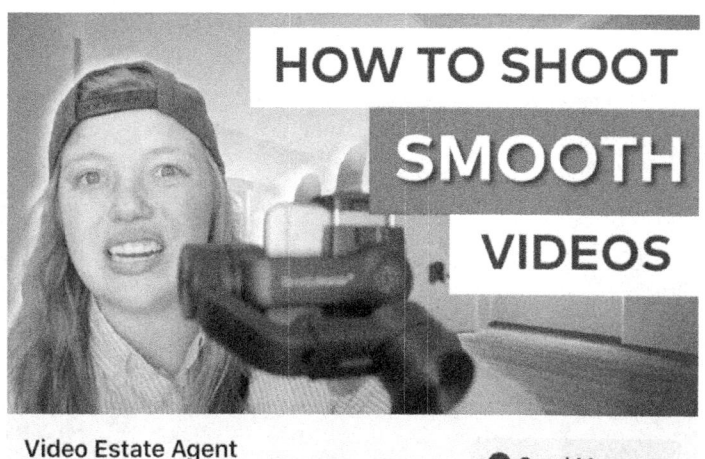

Video Estate Agent
1d

It's TOUGH getting smooth videos - especially when you're walking around

But! It's actually a pretty easy problem to solve.

Stabilization is a must when it comes to shooting your own videos as it portrays professionalism. ... **See More**

HOW TO SHOOT SMOOTH VIDEOS

Video Estate Agent
Real Estate Service

Send Message

Note that this is not likely to get a ton of impressions, as Facebook really doesn't like it when we try to send people off of the platform. However, those who interacted with your last post will likely see this post, and since they've been primed, they are very likely to interact with the post. The more interactions the post gets, the more people will see it.

To ensure the people who interacted with your first post see this new one, go to the old post and tag them in the comments. You can do this by typing the @ sign and their names. To see the names of all of the people who reacted to the post, just click on the little icons in the bottom right corner and scroll through all of the comments.

Day 5/6/7

Then, the big ender! About 7 days after you posted the YouTube video, you will post the entire virtual tour directly to Facebook.

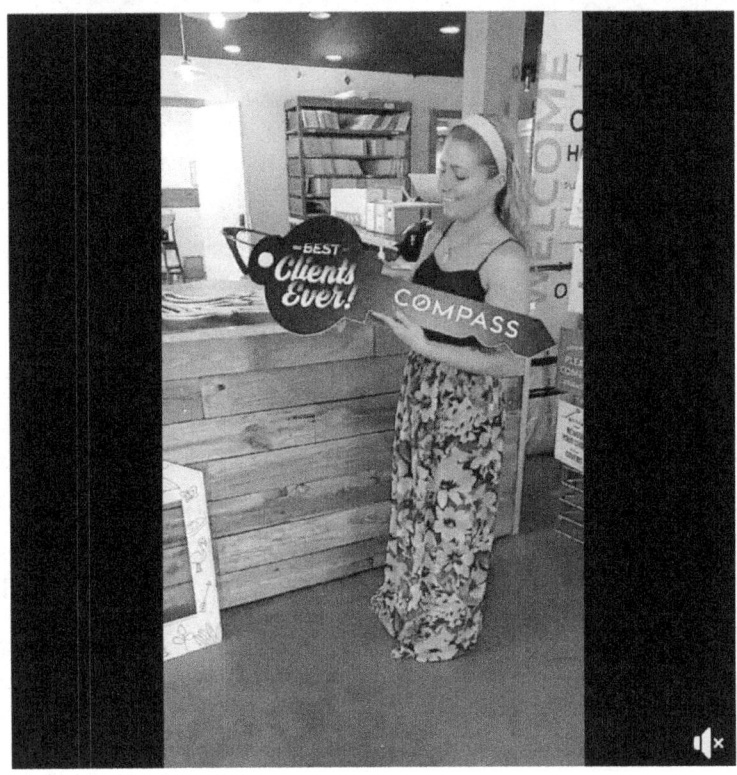

 All Things Real Estate was live.
August 11 at 2:55 PM · 🌐

Custom key time!

Get yours at:
https://allthingsrealestatestore.com/collections/custom

This is Facebook's favorite kind of post because they keep people on Facebook and heavily engaged! That said, this will likely be your best performing post of the three in terms of reach. Most of the people who initially showed interest in the house (those who interacted with the first post) have probably seen the tour already. Still, by seeing it again in this format, they might be reminded of the house or be encouraged to watch the rest of the tour.

On top of reaching all of your existing contacts, Facebook will likely show this video to some new people. Ideally, you will reiterate some of the information you've shared in previous posts (such as the number of rooms, baths, neighborhood, etc.) in the video, so those just seeing the house for the first time will have all the data they need.

BONUS! Target people who watched your video with ads!

After your videos have gone out, you'll want to stay at the forefront of those users' minds. Perhaps the house they saw in the first virtual tour wasn't what they needed, but they are definitely interested in buying (especially if they watched a good portion of your video). A great way to continue to build trust with this audience is to stay in front of them with Facebook Ads.

NOTE: This is a little advanced, if you want a step-by-step video tutorial, go to courses.videoestateagent.com.

Below we will go click-for-click on how to setup an audience you can target with ads.

1. Go to Facebook Ads Manager

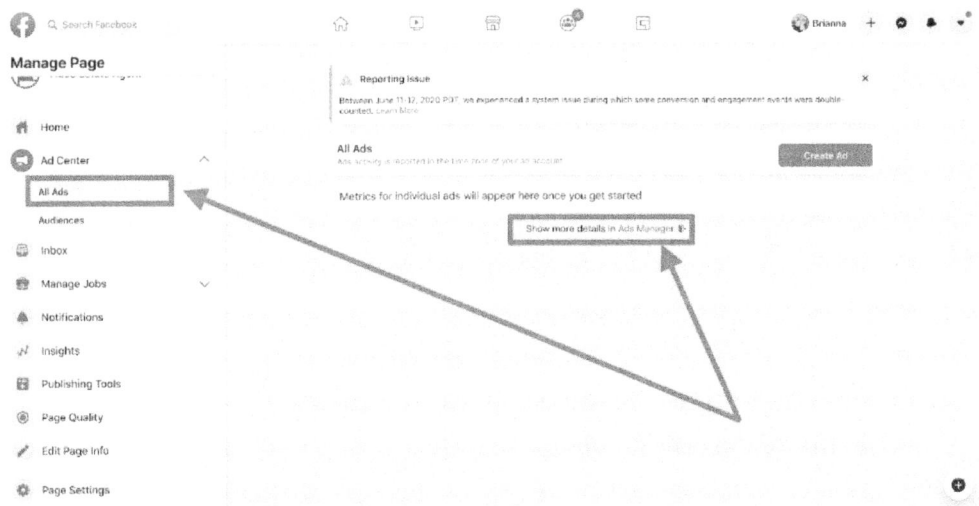

2. Create a new campaign
3. Go to the "ad set" level

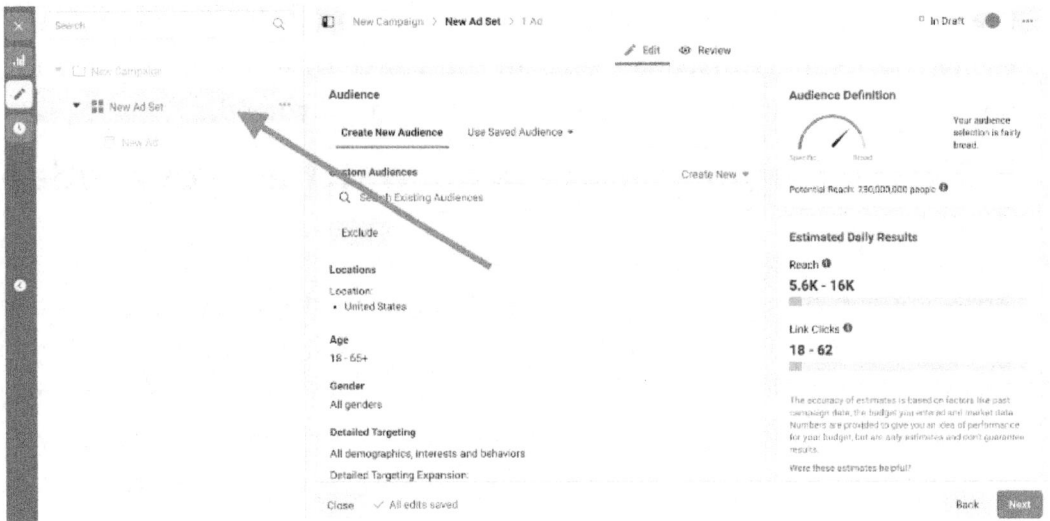

4. Where it says "create new audience" see the line below it
5. Click the "create new" text on the right-hand side

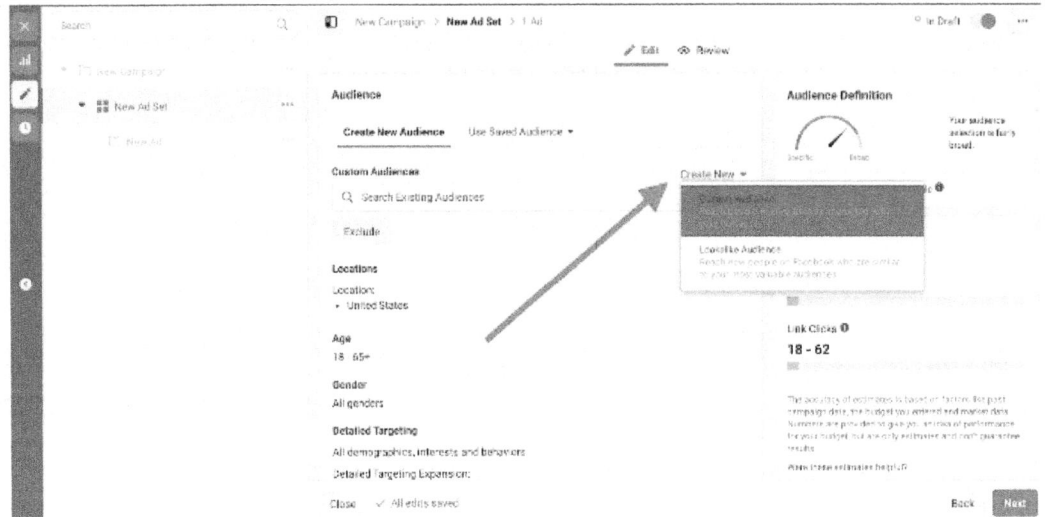

6. From the dropdown select "custom audience"
7. On the next screen select "video"

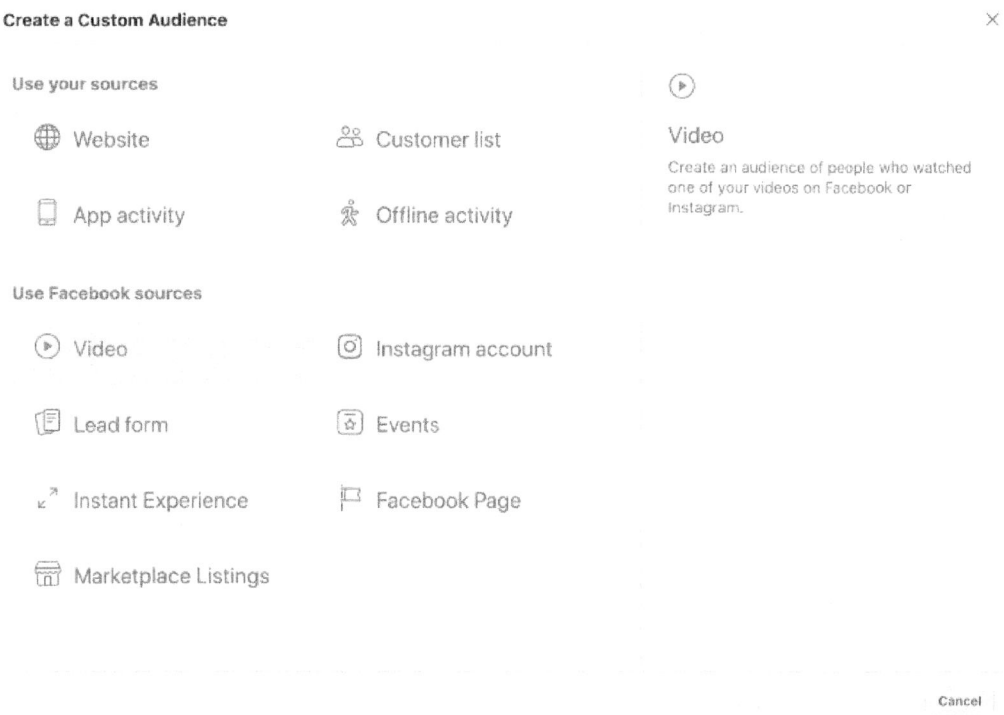

8. Under engagement select "people who viewed at least 10 seconds of your video"

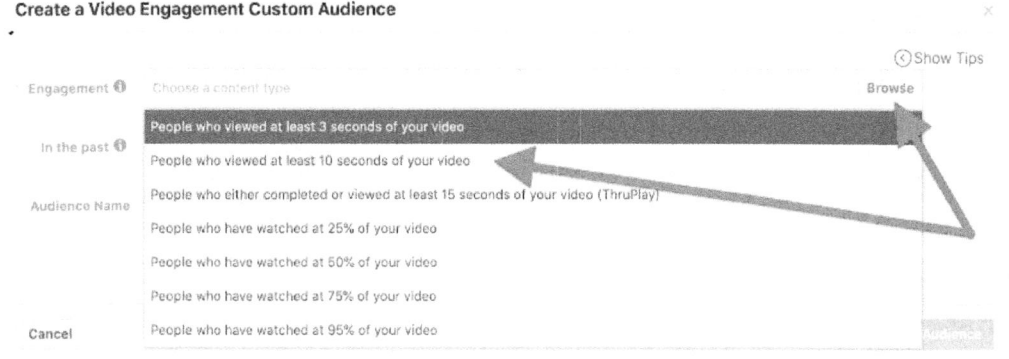

9. OPTIONAL - you can select specific videos if you want by selecting "choose videos"

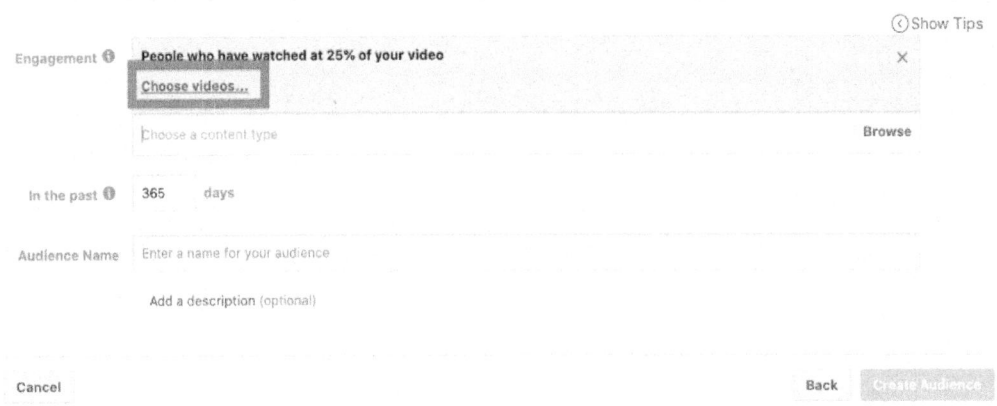

11.   Name your audience

12.   Choose your videos

13.   Select "create audience"

Optional: Instagram/ LinkedIn

Much like Facebook, we strongly suggest you use the short "roll out" method for Instagram and LinkedIn. Both of these platforms have their own unique features that you can add to your overall strategy.

Day 3/4

Again, much like Facebook, the first time you "post" the full tour on these platforms, we want to encourage you to try to get people to view the tour on YouTube. If the audience has already been primed (and they're looking for the tour), they are more likely to take the extra steps to see it.

Instagram

With Instagram, you'll want to make an announcement "story" to let people know the tour is live on YouTube. You will also want to post a short clip of the tour on your feed. In the caption of the video, be sure to list the specs of the house, mention that the full video is on YouTube, and add a few local hashtags (such as #wichitalifeict). Again, be sure you tag the proper location in the post.

When you post this to Instagram, you will also want to make sure that you put the YouTube link in your bio. This is because Instagram doesn't currently support hyperlinks in their captions!

LinkedIn

On LinkedIn, the best way to get traction is to stick to the following format:

- Hook (biggest selling point)
- Additional information (house specs)
- Call-to-action (View the full video on YouTube)
- Three hashtags

With that text, you will want to add a short clip of the tour or another group of photos.

Day 5/6/7

Instagram

On Instagram, you can upload the full video to IGTV. When you post this, we suggest following the same captioning method (minus mentioning the YouTube link) and sharing the post to your IGTV.

LinkedIn

On LinkedIn, you're limited to videos that are 10 minutes long. If your virtual tour is shorter than 10 minutes, we suggest posting the entire video using a similar format as your last post. The hook could be something as simple as "It's finally here 🏡" and the additional information could be some of the location specific information.

Step 5: Website

You absolutely want to show your excellent agent virtual tours on your website so that you can get them in front of potential clients.

Ideally, you will have a place on your website where you show off all of your listings - if that is the case, this is the perfect place to share your tour video. To do this, you will need to get with the person who manages your website and give them the link to your YouTube video.

Once you've got your video on your website (about seven days after you've posted it to YouTube), we suggest directing your audience to your website to watch the full tour. This limits distractions and gives the audience a deeper connection with you and your brand.

Download the following worksheets at: videoestateagent.com/virtual-tour-downloadables

VIDEO MARKETING STRATEGY

7 - 10 DAYS BEFORE
Create a Facebook event for live virtual open houses

WEEK BEFORE
Foster engagement in your Facebook event DAILY

DAY 0
Post your full video (or go live) to your Facebook Page
Share your post to your Facebook Profile

DAY 1
Post full edited video to YouTube and MLS
Reach out to all people who attended live event

DAY 3
Post "preview" to Facebook (Page and Profile), LinkedIn and/or Instagram
Encourage people to view full video on YouTube
Send link to your email list

DAY 5
Put out a "teaser" video that has 1-2 clips in it on Facebook, Instagram, and/or LinkedIn

DAY 7 - 10
Post full video to Instagram and/or LinkedIn and follow up with all interested parties

WHAT GOES WHERE?

Facebook	YouTube
• Long form live videos • Short form (1.5 - 3 minute) videos • Teaser videos (<30 seconds) • Videos for people in your network	• Edited long form videos • Any videos you plan to share on other social sites • Videos you want found by people outside of your current audience

LinkedIn	Instagram
• Videos that are engaging to a higher end audience • Videos that show off your sales skills, offer a bit of educational information or include another professional	• Videos that really catch the eye • Short form videos (less than 60 seconds) • Looking to reach locals outside of your network

Email	Website
• Videos that are showing off a home to a warm audience • Share as links to your YouTube videos that are less than 5 minutes long	• Virtual Tour • For people interested in that specific home

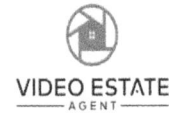

VIDEO ESTATE
— AGENT —

NOTE SHEET

Conclusion

Obviously, I've grown a lot since the days of being chewed out by a red-faced Frank Messina. However, I never forgot the lesson I learned that day as he pointed to that wayward car in my photo:

"Agents who cut corners are a dime a dozen."

In my subsequent years in real estate, I was able to expand on this lesson through my own experiences. I learned more about what it takes to be successful, what clients want, and – more importantly - what they EXPECT. I learned how thinking about and planning even the simplest of tasks can end up creating a much better (and much more profitable) result.

Today, our industry is facing one of the toughest challenges in its history. Not only has the COVID-19 pandemic virtually eliminated our ability to sell the way we know how, but it has accelerated our industry's transition into a cold, digital medium. If we're lucky, the pandemic will end soon enough. However, we can pretty much forget about real estate going back to "normal."

The votes are in: Zoom, Facebook Live, and Instagram are the new normal now. In order to succeed in this industry, we need to know how to use these platforms. More than that, we need to know how to leverage them so that both our personalities and the warmth we bring to client interactions show through.

In this book, we've done our best to give you a detailed crash course in how to do that. Whether you're a tech expert just getting started in real estate or a stubborn boomer still clinging to her flip phone – this book has everything you need to start this all-important transition now.

While I can't tell you what the future hold for the real estate industry, I can tell you that people will never stop buying homes, apartments, businesses, and property. However, the way they do so (and the way we help them) will change just as it always has. With this guide at your side, you have the tools and advice you need to get ahead of that change and the best real estate agent you can be.

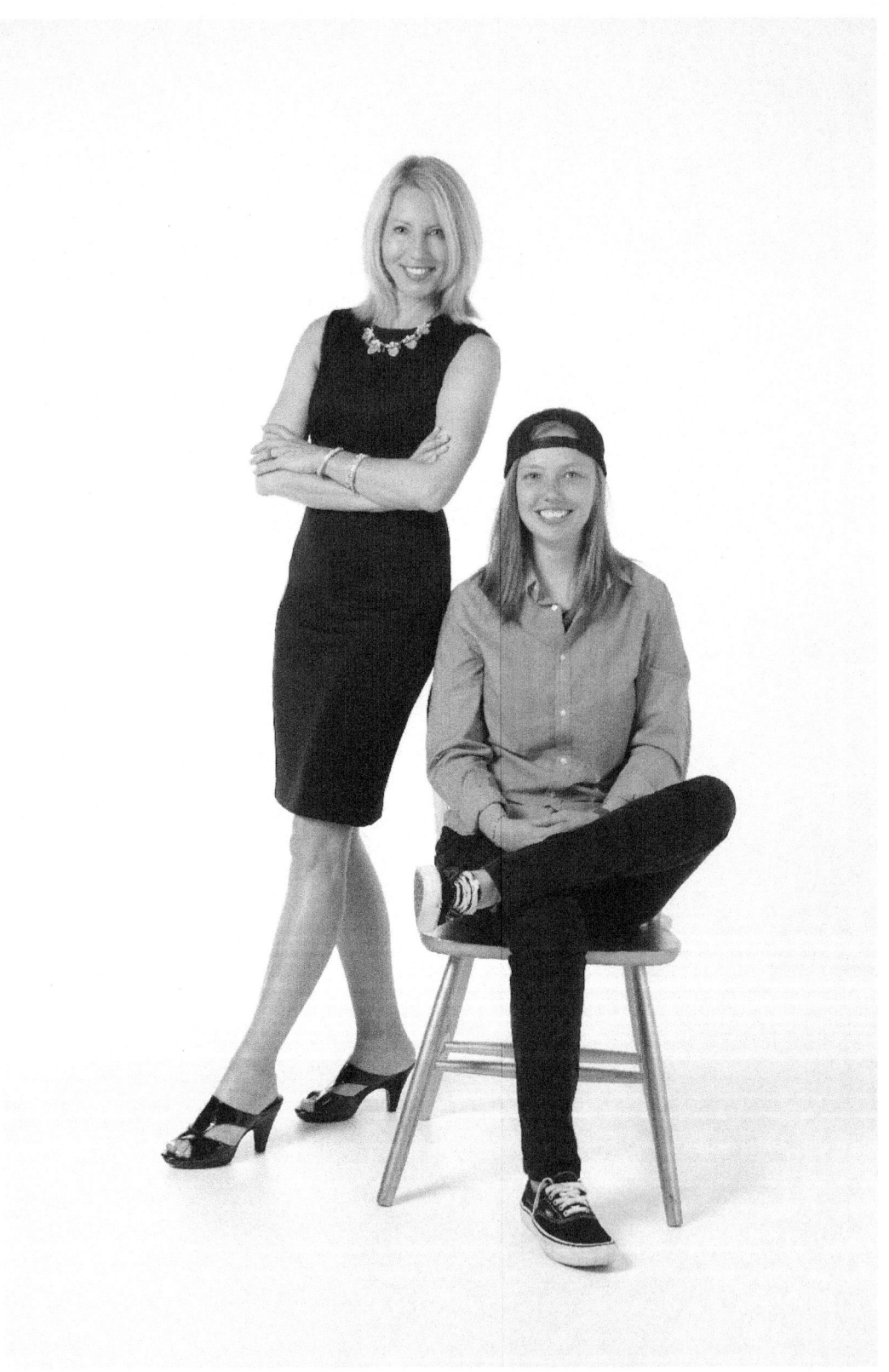

ABOUT THE AUTHORS

Brie E. Anderson is a seasoned digital marketer. She received her degree in Social Media Marketing from Western Kentucky University. During her college years, she had four internships - she was determined to learn as much as she possibly could. Before graduating, she secured a job at an agency in Wichita, Kansas, where she moved two weeks after graduation! At the agency, she was privileged enough to work with clients like the best franchise to buy (as named by Forbes), Freddy's Frozen Custard, one of the leading aviation companies in the world, Textron Aviation, the school she now teaches at, WSU Tech, and over 40 other clients. During this time, Brie handled over $500,000 in search engine optimization work, multiple social media campaigns and over $2 million in digital ad spend. Today, Brie is owner of BEAST Analytics, her digital marketing analytics and strategy consultancy.

Tracy Ramsay has been a Realtor® for over twenty years and was consistently in the top three percent of agents in her market. She maintains her real estate license, invests in income property, and is CCA-Certified Coach. She works as a sales/accountability coach for The Carnahan Group, Reece Nichols, South Central Kansas. Tracy has a Bachelor's Degree in Speech Communication Studies from Hamline University, Minnesota, and a Master's Degree in Communication from University of Northern Iowa. During graduate school, she taught in the speech communication department.

Claim Your Free Worksheets!

Go to the super-secret page,
https://videoestateagent.com/book-downloadables/ and use the
password: MoreViews

Then download the worksheets by clicking the "download" buttons.

Create Your Persona
www.realestatepersonabuilder.com.

Enroll in a Video Estate Agent Course
Go to courses.videoestateagent.com and purchase the course best for
you.

Find Video Estate Agent on Social Media
https://www.facebook.com/VideoEstateAgent
https://www.instagram.com/videoestateagent/
https://www.youtube.com/channel/UCcYnYXa-rTKrdELZ1p3489w
https://www.pinterest.com/videoestateagent/

End Notes

[1] National Association of Realtors®. (2020). https://www.nar.realtor/.

[2] Taylor, Candace. "Coronavirus Has Some Buyers Purchasing Homes Without Setting Foot Inside Them," The Wall Street Journal, May 14, 2020, https://www.wsj.com/articles/coronavirus-has-some-buyers-purchasing-homes-without-setting-foot-inside-them

[3] Royster, Kathryn. "Real Estate Video Marketing's Biggest Return on Investment: High-Quality Community and Listing Videos Syndicated to YouTube, Shared on Social," Inman, July 7, 2014, https://www.inman.com/next/by-the-numbers-how-to-focus-your-video-marketing-for-the-biggest-return-on-investment/.

[4] Royster, "Real Estate Video Marketing," Inman.

[5] Wong, Rachel. "A Realtors®® Guide to Video Marketing," RESAAS Blog (RESAAS, June 22, 2017), https://blog.resaas.com/articles/video-marketing-guide-for-Realtors®-infographic.

[6] Wong, "Realtors® Guide," RESAAS Blog.

Made in the USA
Coppell, TX
26 August 2022

82076421R00098